Public Speaking

From Stage Fright to Spotlight

Calm your fear and anxiety, captivate the audience and command any room with confidence, even if you've never been on stage before!

A. McKeown

©Copyright Anne McKeown 2024 - All rights reserved.

The content within this book may not be reproduced, duplicated or transmitted without direct written permission from the author or the publisher.

Under no circumstances will any blame or legal responsibility be held against the publisher or author for any damages, reparation, or monetary loss due to the information contained within this book. Either directly or indirectly. You are responsible for your own choices, actions, and results.

Legal Notice:

This book is copyright-protected. This book is only for personal use. You cannot amend, distribute, sell, use, quote or paraphrase any part of the content within this book without the consent of the author or publisher.

Disclaimer Notice:

Please note the information contained within this document is for educational and entertainment purposes only. We have made every effort to present accurate, up-to-date, and reliable information. No warranties of any kind are declared or implied. Readers acknowledge that the author is not engaging in the rendering of legal, financial, medical or professional advice. The content within this book has been derived from various sources. Please consult a licensed professional before attempting any techniques outlined in this book.

By reading this document, the reader agrees that under no circumstances is the author responsible for any losses, direct or indirect, which are incurred as a result of the use of the information contained within this document, including, but not limited to, — errors, omissions, or inaccuracies.

Empowering Publications

Contents

1. The Power of Public Speaking — 1
2. Conquering Your Fear of Public Speaking — 3
3. Finding Your Distinct Public Speaking Voice — 19
4. Crafting Compelling Content — 32
5. Mastering the Art of Storytelling — 46
6. Body Language and Nonverbal Communication — 61
7. Vocal Techniques for Maximum Impact — 74
8. The Art of Audience Engagement — 86
9. Effective Use of Technology and Visual Aids — 101
10. Tailoring Your Message Across Various Contexts — 113
11. Specialized Techniques for Different Audiences — 127
12. Pursuing Growth as a Public Speaker — 139
13. Setting Yourself Apart as a Public Speaker — 151
14. Final Word — 164

1

THE POWER OF PUBLIC SPEAKING

"Words have incredible power, they can make people's hearts soar."
M Grothe

Public Speaking is the greatest fear for 77% of the population.[1] It can be terrifying to have the spotlight on you. Just the thought of it makes most people feel vulnerable, judged and inadequate. So why would anyone put themselves through that? Why would I write a book encouraging you to do that?

Because public speaking is liberating!

Public speaking offers an opportunity to open hearts and minds, highlight biases, educate, inspire, and motivate change. The personal and professional growth that takes place when you step out of your comfort zone and put yourself forward to share your ideas and knowledge is unparalleled. Public speaking can be fun when viewed through a positive lens. It is also gratifying when you get it right and receive favorable feedback. Public speaking is powerful, and it is a privilege.

My sincere hope for you, the reader, is that by the time you've finished this book, you will be excited about delivering speeches and presentations

---

1. Furmark T, Tillfors M, Everz P, Marteinsdottir I, Gefvert O, Fredrikson M. Social phobia in the general population: prevalence and sociodemographic profile. *Soc Psychiatry Epidemiol.* 1999;**34**(8):416–424.

of every kind. You will use anxiety as a positive stress, squash all limiting beliefs, craft great stories with ease, take command of any stage with confidence, share what you have learned with others, and most importantly, have fun!

This is a step-by-step guide where each chapter builds on the previous one, so I encourage you to read it chronologically. Some experienced speakers may prefer to dip in and out of chapters, depending on the resources they are looking for. You may notice some topics or suggestions repeated in a few chapters. For example, 'seeking feedback from peers and mentors' is useful and relevant when working on your natural strengths, core message, unique voice, and delivery style; all of these topics are individual chapters. I have endeavored to put a different slant on any repeated key lessons or suggestions. I know from experience that repetition is beneficial when learning something new.

My journey to public speaking mastery has spanned over 25 years of coaching individuals and teams from all walks of life. I've worked with large corporations, small businesses, government departments and local storytellers. Drawing from disciplines like Neuro Linguistic Programming, Positive Psychology, and Chaplaincy, I've developed a holistic approach that addresses the roots of our fears while providing practical strategies to build real confidence and captivating presentations and speeches.

In this book, you'll embark on a transformative path from a nervous novice to a masterful speaker who can engage any audience. We'll explore techniques and the psychology behind public speaking anxiety. We'll look at how to retrain your conscious and unconscious mind so they work in your favor. You'll gain insights into leveraging your personality and adapting to diverse cultural contexts.

Whether you're planning a business pitch, preparing a wedding speech, or just looking to write and share an inspiring story, this book is for you. Questionnaires and checklists are included to help you every step of the way. So, let's get started...

2

CONQUERING YOUR FEAR OF PUBLIC SPEAKING

"Everything you want is on the other side of fear."
J Canfield

Are you terrified of being asked to stand up and give a presentation? Does the mere thought of being in front of an audience, all eyes fixed upon you, send shivers down your spine and make your palms sweat?

If you answered yes, you're not alone. Fear of public speaking, otherwise known as glossophobia, is one of the most common human phobias. But there's good news: with the right strategies and mindset, you can conquer your fears and unlock your full potential as a confident, engaging speaker.

In this chapter, we'll dive into the physiological and psychological origins of public speaking anxiety, differentiate between irrational fears and realistic outcomes, and explore how the brain reacts to the prospect of speaking in front of others. You'll be armed with powerful strategies to diminish fear's hold over you, learn preparation rituals to minimize nervous symptoms, and discover techniques to foster audience engagement and reduce perceived judgment.

By the end of this chapter, you'll have the tools and knowledge needed to face your fears head-on.

The Science of Fear

To conquer your fear of public speaking, it's essential to understand its roots. When faced with speaking in front of an audience, your body's sympathetic nervous system kicks into high gear, triggering the fight, flight or freeze response. This evolutionary mechanism, designed to protect you from perceived threats, releases adrenaline and cortisol, leading to physical symptoms like sweating, shaking, and a racing heartbeat.

However, the origins of public speaking anxiety go beyond mere physiology. Psychologically, the fear often stems from a deep-seated need for approval and acceptance. The prospect of judgment, criticism, or rejection from an audience can be incredibly daunting, triggering feelings of self-doubt and inadequacy. This fear is further compounded by the spotlight effect, a cognitive bias that leads us to believe that others are paying more attention to us than they are.

At its core, stage fright is rooted in fear of the unknown and fear of failure, both of which trigger our body's default stress responses. This fear is not just about speaking in front of an audience but is deeply tied to our sense of self and our desire to be viewed favorably by others. It's the dread that a single mistake could undermine our credibility or embarrass us in front of our peers. This intense anxiety can be debilitating, but understanding that this fear is a natural human response is the first step toward managing it. Knowledge about the psychological triggers of stage fright, such as feeling out of control, being the center of attention, and fearing negative evaluation, can demystify this fear and reduce its power over your psyche.

Irrational Fears vs. Realistic Outcomes

One critical step in overcoming public speaking anxiety is to differentiate between irrational fears and realistic outcomes. Our minds tend to conjure up worst-case scenarios, such as forgetting our speech, being laughed at, or fainting on stage. However, these catastrophic outcomes are rarely, if ever, realized.

In reality, audiences are generally forgiving and understanding. Most people are glad it's you on the stage and not them. They want you to succeed and are not there to judge or criticize you. Minor mistakes, like stumbling over a word or losing your place, are often barely noticed by others and are quickly forgotten. By putting your worries into perspective and recognizing the unlikelihood of your feared outcomes, you can begin to chip away at the power fear holds over you.

Retraining Your Brain

The good news is that our brains are remarkably adaptable. Through neuroplasticity, we can rewire our neural pathways to change how we respond to the prospect of public speaking. Exposure therapy is a powerful technique for retraining your brain, which involves gradually confronting your fear in a controlled, safe environment.

Start by visualizing yourself successfully delivering a speech to a supportive audience. Mentally rehearse your successful performance, picturing yourself speaking confidently, clearly, and passionately. Engage all your senses, imagining the room, the faces of interested listeners, and the sound of your strong voice amid applause. Feel confidence pulse through your body as you lift your chin and straighten your shoulders. As you become more comfortable with this mental rehearsal, gradually expose yourself to increasingly challenging speaking situations, such as practicing in front of a mirror, recording yourself, or speaking to a small group of trusted friends.

Cognitive restructuring is another effective tool for rewiring your brain. This involves identifying and challenging the negative thoughts and beliefs that fuel your anxiety. When you think, "I'm going to make a fool of myself," or "I'm not good enough," take a step back and question the validity of these thoughts.

Use the acronym T.H.I.N.K. to ask yourself, is what I'm thinking and saying to myself: **True? Helpful? Inspiring? Necessary? Kind?**

If the answer to any of these questions is "no," then stop that train of negative thought immediately and replace it with positive, realistic beliefs such as "I am well-prepared and have valuable insights to share" or "The audience is keen to hear what I have to say and wants me to succeed."

Techniques for Reducing Anxiety

Physical relaxation techniques, such as progressive muscle relaxation or gentle stretching, can help calm your body and mind before speaking. Try the following exercises.

> **Physical Relaxation Techniques**
>
> **Neck Stretches**
> - Gently tilt your head towards your shoulder and hold for 8-10 seconds. Repeat on the other side. Slowly roll your head in a full circle twice, then reverse the direction.
>
> **Shoulder Rolls**
> - Lift your shoulders towards your ears and then roll them back, creating large circles. Do 5 rolls backward, then 5 rolls forward.
>
> **Arm Stretches**
> - Extend one arm across your chest, use the other arm to pull it closer, and hold for 10 seconds. Switch arms and repeat.
>
> **Wrist Flexes**
> - Extend your arm, palm up, and gently pull back on the fingers of your extended hand with your other hand. Hold for 5 seconds. Flip your arm so the palm is facing down and gently press down on the back of the hand. Hold for 5 seconds. Repeat with the other arm.

Torso Twists
- Sit or stand with your feet hip-width apart. Gently twist your torso to the right, using your hands to deepen the stretch. Hold for 10 seconds, then twist to the left and hold for another 10 seconds.

Leg Stretches
- While sitting, extend one leg outward and reach toward your toes, holding for 10-15 seconds. Switch legs and repeat.

Deep Breathing
- Close your eyes, place a hand on your abdomen, and slowly inhale through your nose, feeling your stomach rise. Exhale slowly through your mouth, pushing out as much air as you can while contracting your abdominal muscles. Repeat 5 times.

Perform these stretches in a quiet, comfortable space. Focus on your breathing throughout the stretches to enhance relaxation. Don't push into pain; stretches should feel relieving.

Breathing techniques are among the most effective ways to control the physical symptoms of anxiety. Deep belly breathing is particularly beneficial, as it involves breathing deeply and slowly through the abdomen rather than shallowly through the chest. This method counteracts the rapid, shallow breaths that often accompany anxiety, helps lower the heart rate, and promotes a sense of calm.

The breathing technique I use is called box breathing. Try it now by following these simple steps.

Box Breathing Technique

Inhale

- **Action: Breathe in slowly through your nose.**
  Count: 4 seconds.
  Visual Cue: Imagine drawing the first side of a box in your mind.

Hold

- **Action: Keep the air inside.**
  Count: 4 seconds.
  Visual Cue: Visualize drawing the second side of the box.

Exhale

- **Action: Slowly breathe out through your mouth.**
  Count: 4 seconds.
  Visual Cue: Picture drawing the third side of the box.

Hold Again

- **Action: Do not inhale immediately.**
  Count: 4 seconds.
  Visual Cue: Complete the box by drawing the fourth side.

Repeat: Continue this pattern for several minutes until you feel more relaxed.

Anchoring is a powerful technique for strengthening the mind-body connection. An anchor is a physical stimulus you associate with a desired emotional state, like confidence or calm. By consistently pairing your anchor with the desired state during practice, you create a conditioned response you can trigger when speaking. For example, you can use your special speaker shoes as an anchor. Let me explain. Wearing slippers at home signals to the mind and body that it's time to relax. Putting on your runners indicates it's time to work your body and increase your heart rate. Women may wear high-heeled sandals when out socializing, associating them with an evening of dancing and drinking. In the same way, as soon as your feet slip into your nominated speaker shoes, your mind and body know it's time to enter a state of self-assured readiness, and you instantly take on the persona of a capable, confident public speaker.

> **Discover Your Anchor: A Personal Exercise**
>
> By identifying your own personal anchor, you can create a reliable pathway to reach your peak state whenever you need to speak publicly.
>
> **1 Reflect on Comfort and Confidence**
> Think about a time when you felt incredibly confident and at ease.
> What were you doing?
> What objects were around you?
> What actions were you taking?
>
> **2 Choose Your Anchor**
> Select an object or action from your reflection that you can easily replicate or carry with you. This could be anything from a piece of jewelry to a specific gesture.
>
> **3 Write It Down**
> Write down your chosen anchor.
> Describe why this object or action makes you feel confident and how you plan to use it before or during your public speaking engagements.

Set aside time to develop a pre-talk ritual that works for you. By consistently performing your pre-talk routine, you retrain your brain to associate the routine with readiness and confidence, reducing the intensity of nervous symptoms. The connection between mental preparation and physical symptom reduction is powerful. When you feel mentally prepared and confident, your body follows suit, releasing tension and allowing you to present easily.

Pre-Talk Ritual for Public Speaking

Visualization
- **Purpose:** Mentally rehearse your success to create a positive mindset.
- **Method:** Close your eyes for a few minutes and imagine yourself delivering a flawless presentation. Visualize the audience engaging with your content, smiling, and nodding in agreement.

Mindful Meditation
- **Purpose:** Reduce stress and center your thoughts.
- **Method:** Spend 5-10 minutes in meditation. Focus solely on your breathing and let go of distracting thoughts. This practice can ground your emotions and sharpen your focus.

Vocal Warm-ups
- **Purpose:** Prepare your voice for public speaking.
- **Method:** Perform a series of vocal exercises such as humming, lip trills, and tongue twisters. This will help clear your throat and ensure your voice is clear and strong.

Physical Exercise
- **Purpose:** Release tension and increase energy levels.
- **Method:** Engage in light physical activity such as jumping jacks, a quick walk, or stretching. This stimulates blood flow and enhances oxygen supply to your brain.

Review Key Points
- **Purpose:** Solidify your material and boost confidence.
- **Method:** Go over your notes or cue cards and rehearse your opening and closing statements. Familiarity with your material will reduce anxiety and improve delivery.

Set Intentions
- **Purpose:** Align your goals for the presentation.
- **Method:** Write down or mentally note what you wish to achieve with your talk. Focusing on your intentions can help you steer the presentation effectively.

Engage with Early Arrivers
- **Purpose:** Reduce feelings of isolation and build rapport.
- **Method:** If possible, mingle with some of the audience members who arrive early. This can make the environment feel more familiar and less daunting.

Engagement is a potent way to reduce anxiety and perceived judgment and foster a positive connection with your audience. When you actively involve your listeners in your presentation, you shift the focus from yourself to the shared experience, diminishing the intensity of your self-consciousness.

Take the spotlight off yourself and focus on your audience. Choose to serve them and include some of the following techniques to foster engagement.

Engagement Techniques

Ask Questions
- **Description:** Begin with a thought-provoking question to spark curiosity and encourage audience interaction. Tailor questions to the topic and the interests of your audience to maintain relevance. **Example:** "By a show of hands, how many of you have experienced...?"

Share Personal Stories
- **Description:** Share anecdotes and personal experiences to build rapport and add authenticity to your message. Stories can make complex ideas more relatable and memorable. **Example:** "Let me tell you about a time when I was in your shoes..."

Use Humor
- **Description:** Lighten the atmosphere and connect with the audience through appropriate humor. Jokes or amusing remarks can help break the ice and make the content more digestible. **Example:** "Why don't scientists trust atoms anymore? Because they make up everything!"

Maintain Eye Contact
- **Description:** Make eye contact with different members of the audience throughout your presentation. This creates a sense of intimacy and can significantly reduce the feeling of speaking to a crowd. **Example:** "As I look around the room, I see faces of people who are here to make a difference."

Preparation is one of the most effective ways to minimize nervous symptoms before speaking. The more familiar you are with your material, the more confident and at ease you'll feel when delivering it. Dive deep into your topic, gather information, organize your thoughts into a clear, logical structure, and practice, practice, practice.

Real-Life Examples

Throughout history, many renowned speakers have faced moments of audience judgment or skepticism, only to fall back on their thorough preparation and turn those challenges into opportunities for positive engagement. Consider the following examples:

In 1963, Martin Luther King Jr. delivered his iconic "I Have a Dream" speech to over 250,000 people at the Lincoln Memorial. Initially met with some resistance and skepticism, King's powerful oratory and visionary message soon won over the audience, inspiring a nation and galvanizing the Civil Rights Movement.

In his 2005 Stanford commencement speech, Apple co-founder Steve Jobs faced an audience of graduates eager for success tips and career advice. Instead, Jobs shared three deeply personal stories of love, loss, and perseverance. By revealing his vulnerabilities and life lessons, Jobs created a powerful, lasting impact on his listeners, transcending preconceived notions or judgments.

A less famous example from my experience as a coach involved a corporate trainer who addressed an initially skeptical audience by inviting them to share their reservations about the new company policy she was there to explain. She disarmed the audience's initial judgment by addressing these concerns directly and integrating their feedback into her presentation. She turned them into active participants in a meaningful dialogue about the policy's implementation.

As these examples illustrate, even in the face of initial audience judgment or skepticism, speakers who approach their listeners with authenticity, vulnerability, and a genuine desire to connect can transform those perceptions into robust, positive engagement.

Remember, your audience is not there to judge you but to learn from you and be inspired by your insights. By providing value, fostering engagement, and approaching your listeners with openness and authenticity, you create a positive, supportive environment that diminishes the power of fear and allows your unique voice to shine through.

The Power of Positive Self-Talk

French Psychologist Émile Coué discovered that his patients recovered more quickly if they repeated optimistic autosuggestions frequently.[1] Over time, the term optimistic autosuggestions has been replaced with positive affirmations, but the idea is the same. Thorough academic research of the power of affirmations began in the late 80s when social psychologist Claude Steele presented Self Affirmation Theory.[2] Positive self-talk and affirmations are among the most effective tools for overcoming stage fright and self-doubt. The way we speak to ourselves has a profound impact on our thoughts, emotions, and actions. By consciously engaging in positive self-talk, we can reshape our mindset and boost our confidence.

I encourage you to develop a set of affirmations that resonate with you and align with your goals as a public speaker.

The following examples are some of my favorites.

---

1. Coué, E. (1922c), "Self Mastery Through Conscious Autosuggestion", pp. 5–35 in Emile Coué, *Self Mastery Through Conscious Autosuggestion*, New York, NY: American Library Service.

2. Steele, C. M. (1988). The psychology of self-affirmation: Sustaining the integrity of the self. Advances in experimental social psychology, 21, 261-302

"I am a confident and capable speaker."
"My message is valuable and deserves to be heard."
"I embrace challenges as opportunities for growth."
"I trust in my preparation and ability to connect with my audience."

Repeat these affirmations regularly, especially in the days leading up to your presentation. Write them down, post them in visible locations, or record yourself saying them and listen to the recording daily. By consistently reinforcing positive self-talk, you gradually rewire your brain to embrace a more confident and self-assured mindset. In moments of self-doubt or anxiety, catch yourself engaging in negative self-talk and actively replace those thoughts with your affirmations. For example, if you think, "I'm going to forget what I want to say," immediately counter that thought with, "I am well-prepared and will deliver my message with clarity and confidence."

Building Resilience and Embracing Failure

Fear of failure is one of the most significant barriers to conquering stage fright. However, it's essential to recognize that failure is inevitable in the growth process. Every successful speaker has experienced setbacks, stumbles, and less-than-perfect presentations. The key is to view these experiences not as defeats but as valuable lessons and opportunities for improvement.

Cultivate a growth mindset by embracing failure as a stepping stone to success. When things don't go as planned, take the time to reflect on what you can learn from the experience. Ask yourself questions like:

What worked well in my presentation?

What areas could I improve upon next time?

How can I use this experience to strengthen my speaking skills?

By approaching failure with curiosity and a willingness to learn, you build resilience and develop the mental fortitude to bounce back from setbacks. Remember that every challenge you face is an opportunity to grow, refine your craft, and become a more effective communicator.

Self-Care and Stress Management

Conquering stage fright and anxiety is not just about the moments you spend on stage; it's also about the way you care for yourself off stage. Engaging in regular self-care practices and effective stress management techniques can significantly impact your ability to manage public speaking anxiety. Prioritize physical self-care by:

1. Getting enough sleep: Aim for 7-9 hours of quality sleep each night to ensure your mind and body are well-rested and prepared for the demands of public speaking.

2. Eating a balanced diet: Fuel your body with nutrient-rich foods that provide sustained energy and support cognitive function.

3. Exercising regularly: Engage in physical activities you enjoy. Exercise helps reduce stress, improves mood, and boosts overall well-being.

Attend to your mental and emotional well-being by:

1. Practicing mindfulness and meditation: Incorporate mindfulness techniques, such as deep breathing and present-moment awareness, to help calm your mind and reduce anxiety.

2. Engaging in hobbies and activities you enjoy: Make time for pursuits that bring you joy and provide a sense of fulfillment outside of public speaking.

3. Surrounding yourself with supportive people: Build a network of friends, family, and colleagues who encourage and uplift you, and don't hesitate to seek support when needed.

Develop effective stress management strategies, such as:

1. Time management and organization: Create a structured plan for your speaking engagements, break tasks down into manageable steps, and allocate sufficient time for preparation.

2. Boundary setting: Learn to say "no" to commitments that overwhelm you or detract from your primary goals as a speaker.

3. Seeking professional support: If your stage fright or anxiety feels overwhelming, consider working with a therapist or coach who specializes in helping individuals overcome public speaking fears.

By prioritizing self-care and implementing effective stress management techniques, you create a strong foundation for managing public speaking anxiety and showing up as your best self when it's time to take the stage.

Mentorship and Community in Overcoming Fear

Conquering stage fright and developing as a speaker is not a journey you must undertake alone. Seeking mentorship and building a supportive community of fellow speakers can be invaluable in overcoming fear and reaching your full potential. Consider reaching out to experienced speakers whose work you admire and respect. Many successful speakers are generous with their time and wisdom and are happy to guide those just starting. A mentor can provide valuable insights, offer constructive feedback, and share strategies for managing stage fright and honing your craft.

In addition to mentorship, surrounding yourself with a community of supportive peers can make all the difference in your growth as a speaker. Attend workshops, conferences, and networking events to connect with other speakers who share your passion and goals. These connections can lead to valuable friendships, collaborations, and learning opportunities from one another's experiences. Create a safe space within your community to share fears, celebrate successes, and offer mutual encouragement. Knowing that you're not alone in your journey and having a network of individuals who understand the challenges and triumphs of public speaking can provide a powerful source of motivation and resilience in the face of fear.

Embracing the Journey

Conquering stage fright and unleashing your potential as a speaker is an ongoing journey of growth, self-discovery, and resilience. As you implement the strategies and mindset shifts explored in this chapter, remember to celebrate your progress and embrace the process. Every small victory, whether delivering a presentation with less anxiety or receiving positive feedback from an audience member, is a testament to your dedication and growth. Acknowledge these wins and use them as fuel to keep moving forward.

Remember that conquering fear is not a one-time event but a continuous practice. There will be moments of doubt and setbacks along the way, but these experiences are all part of the journey. By viewing challenges as opportunities for learning and growth, you cultivate the resilience and adaptability needed to thrive as a speaker.

I encourage you to embrace the journey, trust your preparation, and let your passion for your message guide you.

3

FINDING YOUR DISTINCT PUBLIC SPEAKING VOICE

"The best speeches come from the heart and reflect your passion."
R Robinson

The art of public speaking is about more than fitting into a predefined mold or adhering to a rigid set of rules. It's about discovering the distinct voice within you – a voice shaped by your personality, experiences, and perspectives. The path to becoming a genuinely impactful and unforgettable speaker is paved with self-discovery and the courage to embrace your authentic self. When we speak from a place of authenticity, anchored in our core values and beliefs, we create a profound connection with our audience beyond mere words.

In this chapter, we will embark on a transformative journey of self-exploration, equipped with strategies to help you discover your unique speaking style and harness the power of genuineness to captivate and inspire your listeners. We'll explore the significance of understanding your purpose and tailoring your delivery to align seamlessly with your natural strengths and abilities.

It's time to find your authentic voice and speak with unwavering confidence, firm conviction, and the ability to leave an impact on your audience.

Authenticity: Why Being Yourself Matters

Authenticity has become a rare and valuable commodity in a world saturated with information and competing voices. Audiences crave speakers who are genuine, relatable, and authentic. When you speak from a place of authenticity, you create a sense of trust and connection with your listeners that goes beyond the mere transmission of information.

Authenticity in public speaking is more than honesty or transparency; it's about aligning your words, delivery, and presence with your core values and beliefs. It's about speaking from the heart, sharing your unique experiences and insights, and allowing your personality to shine. When you embrace your authentic self on stage, you permit your audience to do the same, fostering a deeper engagement and rapport.

The benefits of authentic speaking are numerous. First and foremost, authenticity builds trust. When your audience perceives you as genuine and sincere, they are more likely to believe in your message and be open to your ideas. This trust is the foundation upon which all effective communication is built. Authenticity allows you to connect with your audience on a human level. Sharing your own stories, struggles, and triumphs creates a bridge of empathy and understanding. Your listeners see themselves in your experiences and feel a sense of kinship. This emotional connection is what makes your message memorable.

Authenticity is one of the main things that can set you apart from other speakers. In a sea of cookie-cutter presentations and generic messages, a speaker who is unashamedly themselves stands out. Your unique voice, perspective, and style become your competitive advantage, making you memorable and sought-after in your field.

Speaking from a place of authenticity is liberating. When you embrace your true self, you free yourself from the pressure to be perfect or to fit someone else's mold. You can speak confidently, knowing you are being true to yourself and your message. This freedom translates into a more natural, engaging, and impactful performance on stage.

Knowing Your Purpose

First, clarify your purpose to find your authentic voice as a speaker. What is the core message you want to convey to your audience? What change do you hope to inspire, or what action do you want to motivate? By identifying your central theme or objective, you create a guiding light that illuminates your content, delivery, and overall approach.

Start by reflecting on your experiences, passions, and areas of expertise. What topics ignite your curiosity and enthusiasm? What lessons have you learned that could benefit others? What unique perspective do you bring to the conversation? As you explore these questions, look for emerging patterns and themes and use them to craft a clear, compelling core message. For example, if you're passionate about environmental sustainability and have experience implementing green initiatives in your workplace, your core message might be the business case for sustainability. You could share success stories, best practices, and actionable strategies that inspire other leaders to embrace eco-friendly practices in their organizations.

If you've overcome significant challenges in your personal or professional life, your core message might be about resilience and perseverance. You could share your story of overcoming adversity and offer insights and strategies to bounce back from setbacks and achieve success despite the odds.

The key is to identify a message that resonates deeply with you and that you feel compelled to share with others. Your words can move and inspire your audience when you speak with genuine passion and conviction.

Embracing Your Natural Strengths

Each speaker has unique strengths and abilities that shape their delivery style. Some speakers are gifted storytellers; others excel at breaking complex ideas into simple, relatable concepts. To find your authentic voice, identify your natural strengths and tailor your delivery style to align with your congruent self.

One way to identify your natural strengths is to reflect on a time you felt most comfortable and confident speaking in front of others. What were you talking about? How did you structure your message? What kind of feedback did you receive from your audience? For example, if you feel most comfortable sharing personal anecdotes and weaving them into your larger message, storytelling may be one of your natural strengths. You can leverage this strength by incorporating more stories into your presentations and honing your storytelling skills. Or, if you have a knack for breaking down complex ideas into simple, easy-to-understand concepts, your strength may lie in your ability to educate and inform. You can leverage this strength by presenting information clearly and in a structured way, using analogies, examples, and visual aids to make your content accessible and engaging.

Another way to identify your natural strengths is to seek feedback from others. Ask colleagues, friends, or mentors who have seen you speak to share their observations about your style and approach. What do they see as your unique talents and abilities? What do they find most compelling or memorable about your presentations? For instance, if you consistently receive feedback that your passion and enthusiasm are contagious, your strength may lie in your ability to inspire and motivate others. You can capitalize on this strength by focusing on topics that ignite your passion and bringing a high level of energy and conviction to your delivery.

Once you've identified your natural strengths, look for ways to tailor your delivery style to align with them. If humor comes naturally to you, consider incorporating more light-hearted anecdotes or witty observations into your presentations. If you have a talent for painting vivid word pictures, use descriptive language and sensory details to bring your ideas to life.

The key is to embrace what makes you unique and let your authentic personality shine through in your speaking. When you do, your words will have a more significant impact, and your presence on stage will be more powerful and engaging.

Balance Authenticity and Professionalism

While authenticity is crucial, it's equally important to maintain professionalism. Express your true self through a filter of professionalism that respects the audience and the context. Be aware of the appropriate language, humor, and anecdotes for the setting while staying true to yourself.

In situations where your authentic self may not align with the audience's expectations or the event's context, focus on finding common ground. Identify the aspects of your message that resonate with the audience's needs and values and emphasize those points. Adapt your delivery style to suit the context while maintaining the core of your authentic self. For example, if you're a more casual, humorous speaker addressing a formal corporate audience, you might tone down the jokes but keep your warm, relatable demeanor. By striking this balance, you can remain true to yourself while connecting with your audience.

Another way to navigate this balance is to be transparent about your intentions and style. If you know that your approach may be unconventional or unexpected given the context, acknowledge that upfront. You might say, "I know my style is a bit different from what you may be used to, but I promise that my message is relevant and valuable to your work." This transparency can help build trust and rapport with your audience, even if your authentic style doesn't perfectly match their expectations. It shows you respect their needs and perspectives while being true to yourself.

Remember that authenticity doesn't mean oversharing or crossing professional boundaries. While sharing personal stories and experiences is valuable, be mindful of the level of detail and relevance to your more significant message. Avoid sharing anything that might make your audience uncomfortable, or that could undermine your credibility as a speaker. Ultimately, balancing authenticity and professionalism is about being intentional and strategic. It's about finding ways to let your true self shine through while still being respectful and mindful of your audience and the context in which you're speaking.

Letting Go of the Script

Relying too heavily on scripts can hinder your ability to connect with your audience. While it might feel safer to have every word planned, this approach can make your delivery feel stiff and inauthentic. Instead, focus on internalizing your content, understanding it deeply, and speaking from that place of knowledge and conviction.

One way to let go of the script is to practice your presentation multiple times, not to memorize every word, but to deeply understand your key points and the flow of your argument. As you practice, pay attention to the parts of your presentation that feel most natural and authentic. Notice where you tend to ad-lib or go off-script and consider how to incorporate more of that spontaneity into your delivery.

Another strategy is to create a simple outline or roadmap for your presentation rather than a word-for-word script. This approach lets you stay on track and ensure you hit all your key points while leaving room for flexibility.

One technique I use is to create an Acronym for my topic. For example, I use the Acronym I.M.P.A.C.T to talk about the Art of Public Speaking. Each letter reminds me of the subject matter and keeps me on track:

I is for Introduction.
M is for the core Message.
P is for Presentation skills.
A is for Audience engagement.
C is for Confidence.
T is for Technoloy and media tools.

As you become more comfortable with your material, challenge yourself to speak spontaneously for longer. Start with a few minutes of unscripted speaking and gradually build up to more extended periods. This practice will help you develop greater confidence and flexibility as a speaker.

It's also important to remember that letting go of the script doesn't mean abandoning preparation altogether. The more deeply you know your material, the more freedom you have to be authentic and responsive in the moment. By investing time in researching, organizing, and practicing your content, you give yourself the foundation to speak from a place of knowledge and conviction.

Practice and Feedback

Discovering your unique speaking style is an ongoing journey of experimentation and refinement. Seek out opportunities to practice and gather feedback from trusted peers or mentors. Remember, finding your voice is about progress, not perfection. One of the most effective ways to practice is to seek out low-stakes speaking opportunities, such as local Toastmasters clubs, community organizations, or volunteer groups. These environments provide a supportive and encouraging space to try new techniques, hone your skills, and get real-time feedback from your audience. As you practice, experiment with different approaches and styles. Try incorporating more storytelling into one presentation and more data and evidence into another. Play with your vocal variety, pacing, and physical presence on stage. Notice what feels most natural and resonates most with your audience.

Another valuable tool for finding your voice is recording yourself. Use your smartphone or a camera to capture video of your presentations, and then watch them back with a critical eye. Notice your strengths and areas for improvement and look for patterns in your style and approach.

As you review your recordings, ask yourself questions like:

What moments felt most authentic and engaging?

Where did I seem to lose my audience's attention or interest?

How can I make my content or delivery more impactful?

What unique strengths or perspectives do I bring to my speaking?

Be brave and ask colleagues, friends, or mentors who have seen you speak to share their honest observations and insights. Be open to positive and constructive feedback and use it to inform your growth and development as a speaker.

Finally, remember that finding your voice is an ongoing process. As you evolve and grow as a person and a professional, your speaking style will also likely evolve. Be open to this continuous learning and improvement journey, and trust that your authentic voice will emerge more fully with each new experience and opportunity.

Discovering Your Natural Delivery Style: A Speaker's Quiz

1. When preparing for a presentation, I prefer to:

a) Write out a detailed script and rehearse it extensively

b) Create a general outline and trust my ability to improvise

c) Visualize myself delivering the speech and focus on the key messages

2. I feel most energized and engaged when:

a) Interacting directly with the audience and fielding their questions

b) Sharing personal stories and anecdotes that illustrate my points

c) Presenting complex information in a clear, structured manner

3. My natural speaking pace is:

a) Fast and dynamic, with a sense of urgency and excitement

b) Measured and deliberate, with thoughtful pauses for emphasis

c) Adaptable, varying depending on the content and audience

4. When it comes to using humor in my presentations, I:

a) Actively seek opportunities to incorporate jokes and witty observations

b) Use humor sparingly and only when it naturally fits the context

c) Prefer to maintain a more serious, professional tone throughout

5. I feel most authentic and confident when:

a) Inspiring and motivating the audience to take action

b) Educating and informing the audience about a topic I have a passion for

c) Connecting emotionally with the audience through shared experiences

6. When faced with a challenging or skeptical audience, I tend to:

a) Directly address their concerns and engage in open dialogue

b) Focus on delivering my message with conviction and clarity

c) Adapt my approach and find common ground to build rapport

7. My preferred way of incorporating visuals into my presentations is:

a) Using bold, high-impact images and graphics to capture attention

b) Creating simple, clean slides that reinforce critical points without distracting

c) Minimizing visuals and relying primarily on my words and presence

8. When telling a story during a presentation, I aim to:

a) Entertain the audience and leave them with a memorable anecdote

b) Illustrate a lesson or insight that ties back to my core message

c) Create an emotional connection and tap into the audience's empathy

9. I believe the most important aspect of vocal delivery is:

a) Projecting confidence and authority through a robust and clear voice

b) Using vocal variety and inflection to engage and maintain interest

c) Speaking at a pace that allows for understanding and retention

10. When it comes to body language and movement on stage, I:

a) Use expansive gestures and dynamic movement to command attention

b) Prefer a more restrained, controlled approach to convey professionalism

c) Focus on maintaining an approachable presence and open facial expressions

11. I feel most in my element when:

a) Improvising and thinking on my feet during a presentation

b) Delivering a carefully crafted, well-rehearsed speech

c) Engaging in interactive exercises or demonstrations with the audience

12. My ultimate goal as a speaker is to:

a) Inspire the audience to see things in a new way and act

b) Provide practical, actionable insights that the audience can apply immediately

c) Create a memorable, engaging experience that resonates on an emotional level

Interpretation of Quiz Results:

If you scored primarily a's, Your strengths lie in engaging and interacting with the audience. You may thrive in improvisational settings and enjoy using humor and storytelling to create a memorable experience. To improve, focus on structuring your content effectively and practicing a more controlled pace.

Example: If you're naturally inclined to use humor, make sure your jokes are entertaining and relevant to your message. Practicing your timing and delivery can ensure that your humor enhances, rather than detracts from, your content. You might also work on developing a clear roadmap for your presentations to ensure that your engaging style is balanced with a well-structured and purposeful message.

If you scored primarily b's, Your strengths lie in delivering clear, well-structured presentations that educate and inform. You may excel at breaking down complex topics and maintaining a professional presence. To improve, inject more personality and emotion into your presentations, using storytelling and vocal variety to engage your audience.

Example: If you're presenting technical information, consider opening with a personal anecdote that illustrates the human impact of your topic. This can help you connect with your audience more emotionally, making your content more relatable and memorable. You might also experiment with using more vocal variety, such as changing your tone, volume, or pace to emphasize critical points or create a sense of drama and interest.

If you scored primarily c's, Your strengths lie in connecting emotionally with the audience and creating a warm, approachable presence. You may excel at using personal stories and genuine expressions to build rapport. To improve, focus on developing a more structured approach to your content, using clear, vital messages and simple visuals.

Example: If you rely heavily on personal stories, ensure each has a clear purpose and ties back to your main message. Practicing with a well-defined outline can help you balance emotional connection and practical, actionable insights. You might also work on incorporating more data, evidence, or examples to support your key points and give your message greater credibility and impact.

Embracing the Power of Your Unique Voice

Your voice is a powerful tool for connection, persuasion, and transformation. By staying true to yourself, speaking from the heart, and consistently refining your craft, you'll find your authentic voice and unlock your full potential as a speaker and leader. Remember, your unique perspective, experiences, and style set you apart and make you valuable as a speaker. Embrace what makes you different, and trust that your authentic voice is precisely what your audience needs to hear.

Be patient and kind with yourself as you continue on your public speaking journey. Celebrate your successes, learn from mishaps, and keep pushing yourself to grow and evolve. The more you practice and speak from a place of authenticity, the more powerful and impactful your voice will become. Take a deep breath, step onto the stage, speak your truth, and watch as your words ignite the hearts and minds of those who have the privilege of listening.

Your voice is your power – use it wisely.

4

CRAFTING COMPELLING CONTENT

"Speech content is crafted to persuade, convert and compel."
R Emerson

Crafting compelling content is the foundation of delivering a presentation that informs, persuades, and inspires. In this chapter, we will look at ways to make your presentation engaging by developing a captivating hook, defining your core message, structuring your speech effectively, and using repetition techniques to emphasize your key points and leave a lasting impression.

Structuring for Success

A compelling presentation relies on a clear and effective structure to support its content and ideas. With a well-defined framework, your audience can quickly understand your message. A classic presentation structure follows the "Tell them what you're going to tell them, tell them, then tell them what you told them" Approach, which involves:

1. Opening with a clear introduction that previews your core message and main points.
2. Delivering the body of your presentation, exploring each of your main points in depth.
3. Concluding with a summary of your key takeaways and a call to action for your audience.

Engaging Introductions

Your introduction is your opportunity to capture your audience's attention, establish your credibility, and provide a preview of the content you will be presenting. A strong introduction should:

1. Begin with an attention-grabbing statement: start with a surprising statistic, a thought-provoking question, or a powerful story that immediately captures your audience's interest. For example, "The average person spends 90,000 hours at work, over a third of our waking lives. How can we make that time more meaningful, fulfilling, and impactful?"

2. Establish credibility: share a brief anecdote or qualification demonstrating your expertise and authority on the topic. For instance, "As a career coach who has worked with thousands of professionals over the past decade, I have witnessed the transformative power of finding purpose and passion in your work."

3. Preview your core message and main points: give your audience an overview of what they can expect from your presentation, highlighting your key takeaways. For example, "Today, I will share three strategies for crafting a career that aligns with your values, leverages your strengths, and positively impacts the world around you."

The next step is to create a presentation that genuinely resonates with your listeners, which starts with defining your core message and building your content around it with clarity and engagement.

Defining Your Core Message

Every excellent presentation has a clear, concise, and compelling core message. This is the single idea that you want your audience to remember and take away from your speech. Your core message is the foundation of your content creation process, supporting every story, statistic, and argument you include in your presentation.

To define your core message, ask yourself: What is the one thing I want my audience to know, feel, or do as a result of hearing my speech? This could be a call to action, a shift in perspective, or a key takeaway that will help them personally or professionally. For example, suppose you're giving a presentation on the importance of innovation in the workplace. In that case, your core message might be: "Fostering a culture of innovation is crucial for staying competitive in today's fast-paced business landscape, and it starts with empowering employees to think creatively and take calculated risks."

This core message accomplishes several key things:

1. It clearly states the central idea of your presentation: the importance of innovation in the workplace.

2. It highlights the stakes: staying competitive in a rapidly changing business environment.

3. It offers a specific call to action: empowering employees to think creatively and take calculated risks.

4. It suggests the solution is achievable: anyone can foster innovation by starting with small, concrete steps.

A great example is Brene Brown's TED Talk "The Power of Vulnerability." Her core message is that vulnerability is not a weakness but a source of courage, connection, and innovation. This clear, counterintuitive message challenges her audience's assumptions and invites them to rethink their approach to vulnerability.

By crafting a clear, compelling core message, you provide your audience with a roadmap for your presentation and a key takeaway that they can apply to their work and lives.

Ensuring Your Message is Understood

Clarity is essential for making your message stick in your audience's minds. When your ideas are presented in a clear, concise, and easy-to-follow manner, your listeners are more likely to understand, remember, and act on them.

To achieve clarity in your content, focus on:

1. Using simple, jargon-free language that your audience can easily understand.

2. Breaking down complex ideas into smaller, more digestible chunks.

3. Providing examples and analogies to illustrate your points.

4. Repeating key ideas and themes throughout your presentation.

One specific example is Simon Sinek's use of clarity in his TED Talk "How Great Leaders Inspire Action." In this presentation, he:

1. Uses simple language to introduce the concept of the Golden Circle and its three components (Why, How, What).

2. Breaks down the complex idea of leadership and motivation into the simple framework of the Golden Circle.

3. Provides examples of companies like Apple and the Wright brothers to illustrate how starting with "Why" can lead to innovation and success.

4. Throughout the presentation, he repeats the phrase, "People don't buy what you do; they buy why you do it," reinforcing his core message.

By employing these clarity techniques, Sinek has become one of our time's most popular and influential speakers. His TED Talk garnered over 50 million views, and his ideas were widely adopted across industries and sectors.

Making Intricate Topics Accessible

When dealing with complex topics that your audience might need to become more familiar with, it is essential to strike the right balance between complexity and simplicity. While delving into intricate details can showcase your expertise, it can overwhelm your listeners if not handled carefully.

The power of simplicity lies in its ability to make your information more accessible and memorable for your audience. By distilling your content to its most essential elements, you make it easier for your listeners to grasp and retain your key points long after the presentation.

To simplify complex topics effectively:

1. Determine what your audience needs to know versus what is just supplementary information. Focus on the most critical information to convey the big picture and achieve your presentation's goals.

2. Adopt a step-by-step approach. Begin by outlining your topic's main components, then gradually unpack each one logically. This helps your audience follow along and understand the progression of your ideas.

3. Use analogies and examples to make abstract concepts more relatable. Choose comparisons that are relevant and easily understood by your specific audience.

4. Incorporate interactive elements directly related to the simplified concepts you're discussing. This helps make the abstract ideas more concrete and demonstrates how they apply in real-world situations.

It's important to note that simplifying your presentation means eliminating only some essential details. It's about strategically refining your message to focus on the most critical information, breaking down complex ideas into manageable parts, and using tools like analogies to make the content more accessible and engaging. When you strike the right balance between simplicity and substance, your audience will leave feeling like they truly grasp the subject matter and will have a positive impression of your ability to communicate complex ideas in an effective and relatable way.

Making Your Points Memorable

The "Rule of Three" is a well-established principle in various fields, including writing, public speaking, and psychology. Organizing your presentation around three main points makes your message more compelling and memorable for your audience.

When structuring your content, consider how you can break down your core message into three key points or arguments. Each point should be distinct yet interconnected, building upon the previous one to create a cohesive and compelling narrative. For example, if your core message is about the importance of self-care, your three main points might be:

1. The physical benefits of self-care: improved health, energy, and resilience.

2. The mental and emotional benefits of self-care: reduced stress, increased happiness and better relationships.

3. Practical strategies for incorporating self-care into daily life: setting boundaries, prioritizing sleep, and engaging in hobbies.

In his product launch presentation, Elon Musk introduced Tesla's Powerwall battery system by focusing on three key benefits: cost savings, energy independence, and environmental sustainability. This simple, memorable structure helped emphasize the product's value proposition and potential impact.

Reinforcing Your Core Message

As mentioned above, repetition is a necessary and powerful tool for reinforcing your ideas and ensuring that your message sticks. When you repeat your core message throughout your presentation, you signal to your audience that this is the most crucial takeaway they should remember. The key is to find creative ways to weave your core message into your content without sounding dull and repetitive. This can be done through:

1. Reiterating your core message at critical points in your presentation (e.g., in your introduction, transitions, and conclusion).

2. Using different language, examples, or stories to illustrate your core message in new ways.

3. Incorporating rhetorical devices like anaphora (repeating a word or phrase at the beginning of successive clauses), "Every day, we face a choice. Every day, we decide who we want to be. Every day, we have the power to make a difference." Or epistrophe (repeating a word or phrase at the end of successive clauses) to emphasize your message. "In times of hardship, we must persevere. In moments of doubt, we must persevere. When faced with seemingly insurmountable obstacles, we must persevere."

By strategically repeating your core message throughout your presentation, you ensure that your audience walks away with a clear understanding of your central idea and its importance.

Leaving a Lasting Impression

The conclusion of your presentation deserves just as much thought and preparation as the opening. Your closing remarks reinforce your core message and directly impact your audience's ability to retain and act upon what you've shared. An impactful conclusion does more than signal that you're done speaking. It ties all the preceding information together in a cohesive, memorable way. Your audience's minds will be pulled in many directions after your talk, so having a robust, well-constructed close can mean the difference between your message getting lost or sticking with people.

A powerful conclusion should:

1. Summarize your key takeaways: recap the main points of your presentation, reinforcing your core message.

   For example, "Crafting a fulfilling career requires self-reflection, strategic planning, and a willingness to take risks. By identifying your values, leveraging your strengths, and pursuing meaningful opportunities, you can create a professional path that aligns with who you are and what you stand for."

2. Leave your audience with a call to action: give your listeners concrete steps to apply your ideas to their lives or work.

   For instance, "Take some time next week to reflect on your values, passions, and strengths. Write them down, share them with a trusted friend or mentor, and start brainstorming ways to incorporate them into your career. Remember, small steps can lead to big changes over time."

3. End with a memorable statement or story: close your presentation with a thought-provoking quote, a robust statistic, or a personal anecdote that ties back to your core message.

For example, "As the poet Rumi once said, 'Let yourself be silently drawn by the strange pull of what you love. It will not lead you astray.' Trust that pull, and let it guide you toward a career that lights you up. Thank you."

By crafting a powerful conclusion summarizing your key points, inspiring action, and leaving a lasting impact, you ensure that your message resonates with your audience long after your presentation ends.

Storyboarding for Crafting Content

Visualizing the flow and structure of your presentation using a storyboard can be incredibly helpful as you begin to craft your content. A storyboard is a graphic organizer that allows you to plan your content slide by slide or section by section.

To create a storyboard, start by breaking down your presentation into its key components:

Introduction
Main Point 1
Main Point 2
Main Point 3
Conclusion

For each component, outline the key ideas, examples, and visuals you want to include. This could involve writing bullet points, creating rough sketches, or using sticky notes to rearrange and refine your content.

Storyboarding allows you to see your presentation as a cohesive whole, ensuring that each element builds upon the last and supports your core message. It also helps you identify gaps or redundancies in your content to streamline and optimize your presentation for maximum impact.

As you storyboard, keep the following tips in mind:

1. Focus on your core message: ensure every storyboard element supports your central idea.

2. Prioritize clarity and simplicity: use clear, concise language and visuals that support your message without overwhelming your audience.

3. Incorporate variety: alternate between different types of content (e.g., stories, statistics, examples) to keep your audience engaged.

4. Build opportunities for interaction: consider where you might include questions, polls, or activities to involve your audience in the learning process.

Storyboarding is also a powerful tool for unleashing your creative potential in public speaking. Each frame of your storyboard allows you to experiment with different narrative techniques, such as storytelling, analogies, or demonstrations. It's not just about planning what you will say but how you will say it.

Storyboarding can be particularly helpful when you need help or more inspiration. Sketching out your presentation visually can help kick your brain into high gear, engaging different cognitive muscles and helping you make new connections and spark fresh ideas.

Storyboards provide a unique and efficient way to gather and incorporate valuable insights before finalizing your speech. Sharing your storyboard with colleagues or mentors gives them a clear overview of your planned presentation and invites constructive feedback on your talk's structure, content, and flow. This feedback can then be directly applied to the storyboard, allowing you to rearrange, add, or remove elements as needed. This process ensures that your final presentation is as strong, coherent, and impactful as possible.

Overcoming Challenges in Content Creation

Crafting compelling content is rarely straightforward. Even experienced speakers can face challenges such as writer's block, dealing with complex topics, or adapting content for different audiences. Let's explore these common challenges and look at some practical strategies for overcoming them.

Writer's block is a common challenge that can strike at any stage of the content creation process. When you find yourself struggling to generate ideas or put your thoughts into words, try these strategies:

1. Freewriting: set a timer for 10-15 minutes and write continuously without stopping to edit or censor yourself. This can help you bypass your inner critic and get your creative juices flowing.

2. Mind mapping: start with your core message or topic in the center of a blank page, then branch out with related ideas, examples, and stories. This visual brainstorming technique can help you generate new ideas and see connections between different aspects of your topic.

3. Change your environment: sometimes, a change of scenery can help break through writer's block. Try working in a different room, walking, or writing at different times to shake up your routine and stimulate new ideas.

By being proactive and flexible in your approach to content creation, you can overcome common challenges and craft presentations that resonate with any audience. The key is to stay focused on your core message while adapting your content and delivery to your listeners' specific needs and interests. Remember, crafting compelling content is a skill that can be learned and refined over time. The more you practice, the more you'll develop your unique style. Every presentation is an opportunity to educate and entertain your audience. With the right tools and techniques, you have the power to create content that not only communicates your ideas but also sparks meaningful change in the lives of your listeners.

Crafting Compelling Content: A Checklist for Speakers

1. Define your core message:

- Identify the central idea or takeaway you want your audience to remember
- Ensure your core message is clear, concise, and compelling
- Align all your content to support and reinforce this core message

2. Analyze your audience:

- Research your audience's demographics, psychographics, and prior knowledge
- Identify their expectations, needs, and potential objections
- Gather information through surveys, interviews, focus groups, and social media

3. Structure your presentation:

- Use the "Tell them what you're going to tell them, tell them, then tell them what you told them" Approach
- Craft an engaging introduction that captures attention and previews your main points
- Organize your content into clear, logical sections that flow smoothly from one to next
- Create a powerful conclusion that summarizes your key points, inspires action, and leaves a lasting impact

4. Employ the "Power of Three":

- Break down your core message into three main points or arguments
- Ensure each point is distinct yet interconnected and supportive of your central idea
- Use this structure to make your content more memorable and impactful

5. Prioritize clarity and simplicity:

- Use clear, concise language that your audience can easily understand
- Break down complex ideas into smaller, more digestible chunks
- Provide examples, analogies, and visuals to illustrate your points
- Focus on the information that is most critical for achieving your presentation's goals

6. Incorporate storytelling and examples:

- Use stories, case studies & examples to engage and make your ideas more relatable
- Choose examples that are relevant and demonstrate your points in action
- Use different types of content (stories, statistics, examples) to maintain engagement

7. Leverage repetition:

- Repeat your core message throughout your presentation to reinforce its importance
- Use different words, examples, or stories to illustrate your core message in new ways
- Incorporate rhetorical devices like anaphora or epistrophe to emphasize your message

8. Storyboard your presentation:

- Visualize the flow and structure of your presentation using a storyboard
- Use the storyboard to identify gaps, redundancies, or opportunities for improvement
- Seek feedback on your storyboard from colleagues or mentors to refine your content
- Break down your presentation into critical components and outline the main ideas, examples, and visuals

9. Tailor your content to your audience:

- Highlight the aspects of your topic that are most relevant and beneficial to audience
- Address potential objections and provide evidence to support your perspective
- Use the insights from your audience analysis to adapt your language, tone, and delivery style

10. Overcome common challenges:

- Employ analogies, visuals, and examples to break down complex topics
- Be proactive and flexible in adapting your content to different audiences and contexts
- Use strategies like free writing, mind mapping, or changing your environment to overcome writer's block

By following this checklist and incorporating these critical strategies into your content creation process, you'll be well-equipped to craft presentations that educate, engage, and inspire your audience to take action.

So get excited and get started.

5

MASTERING THE ART OF STORYTELLING

"The most powerful person is the storyteller."
S Jobs

Storytelling is a fundamental strategy for creating connection and resonance in public speaking that statistical data alone cannot achieve. The power of storytelling lies in its universal appeal. Humans have told stories since ancient times, finding a shared language transcending individual experiences and technical jargon. As a speaker, you engage your audience intellectually, emotionally, and psychologically using narrative form.

Stories are more than entertainment; they are a fundamental way humans communicate and make sense of the world. A well-told story can illuminate complex ideas, bring abstract concepts to life, and stir emotions that facts alone cannot. When you share a story, you invite your audience to experience reality through your perspective, making the abstract tangible. This connection is invaluable in public speaking, especially when the goal is to persuade, motivate, or inspire.

To understand the impact of storytelling in public speaking, let's look at a couple of real-world examples.

Barack Obama successfully used this technique to engage and inspire audiences during his 2008 presidential campaign. In his speech, "A More Perfect Union," he delivered a groundbreaking message about race relations in America. He used storytelling to address the controversial remarks made by his former pastor, Reverend Jeremiah Wright. He shared his personal story of being born to a black father and a white mother, growing up in a multiracial family, and witnessing both the triumphs and struggles of the African American community.

By weaving his narrative into the larger story of race in America, Obama created a powerful and nuanced speech that addressed a divisive issue with empathy, honesty, and hope.

Oprah Winfrey is regarded as an exceptional public speaker who frequently uses storytelling to captivate her audience and effectively convey her messages. One notable example is her 2018 Golden Globes speech, where she accepted the Cecil B. DeMille Award for lifetime achievement.

In her speech, Oprah shared personal stories highlighting the importance of speaking truth to power and standing up against injustice. She began by recounting her childhood memory of watching Sidney Poitier become the first black man to win an Oscar in 1964. This story set the stage for her to discuss the significance of representation and its impact on her as a young girl. She then transitioned to the story of Recy Taylor, a young African American woman who was raped by six white men in 1944. Despite the challenges, Taylor fought for justice, and her story served as an inspiring example of courage and resilience in the face of adversity.

Through these stories, Oprah emotionally connected with her audience. She used vivid imagery and descriptive language to paint a picture in the minds of her listeners, allowing them to empathize with the characters in her stories.

Oprah's storytelling technique also reinforced her central theme of speaking truth to power. By sharing real-life examples, she demonstrated the impact that individuals can have when they stand up for what is right, even in the face of seemingly insurmountable challenges.

Writing Your Story

Writing your story requires more than a compelling narrative; it demands authenticity and relevance to your core message. As mentioned in the previous chapter, you first must identify the key message or lesson you want your audience to take away. Once clear, think back to experiences in your own life that align with this message. Integrate stories at points in your presentation where you must underscore a particular argument or when the audience needs a break from technical content. Additionally, stories can be used as powerful openers or closers, captivating interest immediately or leaving a lasting impression.

When selecting stories to include in your presentation, consider the following criteria:

1. Relevance: the story should directly relate to your core message and help illustrate or reinforce your key points. Ask yourself, "Does this story contribute to the overall purpose of my presentation, or is it just an interesting anecdote?" Leave it out if the story doesn't support your main arguments or themes.

2. Authenticity: choose genuine stories that reflect your own experiences, values, and beliefs. Audiences can sense when a story feels contrived or inauthentic, which can undermine your credibility as a speaker. When sharing personal stories, be honest about your struggles, failures, and triumphs. This vulnerability can help create a stronger connection with your audience.

3. Emotional impact: select stories that evoke emotions and create a connection with your audience. Stories that elicit joy, surprise, empathy, or inspiration are more likely to be remembered and acted upon. Consider the emotional journey you want to take your audience on and choose stories that support that arc.

4. Conciseness: keep your stories concise and focused, avoiding unnecessary details that can distract from your main message. Aim for stories that can be told in 2-3 minutes or less. If a story is too long or complex, consider breaking it up into more minor anecdotes or focusing on the most essential elements.

When crafting your stories, it's also essential to consider the structure and delivery. A good story should have a clear beginning, middle, and end, a compelling hook that draws the audience in, and a satisfying resolution that ties back to your main message. Use vivid, sensory language to help your audience visualize the events and emotions of the story, and vary your tone, pacing, and volume to create a dynamic and engaging delivery.

Structuring Your Presentation Like a Story

Every compelling story follows a fundamental structure that captivates audiences and keeps them engaged. This structure is a powerful tool in public speaking, especially when sharing complex information. As mentioned before, a good structure involves the following:

1. A clear beginning: set the stage and introduce the central theme. This is where you introduce the characters, establish the setting, and present the central conflict or question that will drive your story forward.

2. A middle: develop the core of your narrative through arguments or points that build upon each other. This is where the story unfolds, with rising action, obstacles, and revelations that keep the audience engaged.

3. An end: provide a resolution. This is where the story reaches its climax, and the central conflict is resolved, leaving the audience with a sense of satisfaction and closure.

Creating a Narrative Arc

The emotional connection that stories forge sets them apart from other forms of communication. While the brain's analytical areas process facts, stories activate parts of the brain involved in experiencing emotions and sensations. To enhance this connection, focus on the emotional arc of your story:

1. How do the characters in your story feel? What are their hopes, fears, and motivations? By making your characters relatable and their emotions palpable, you invite your audience to empathize and become invested in their journey.

2. What challenges do they face, and how do they overcome them? Every good story involves some conflict or obstacle that the characters must navigate. By highlighting the difficulties your characters face and how they rise to meet those challenges, you create a sense of tension and release that keeps your audience engaged.

3. How does their journey mirror the emotions you want your audience to feel? Consider the emotional trajectory you want your audience to experience throughout your presentation. Do you want them to feel inspired, empowered, or curious? Use your story to guide them through those emotional states, creating a shared experience that resonates.

The narrative arc of your presentation should guide your audience through an emotional and intellectual journey. Begin with an introduction that poses a question or presents a challenge that grabs interest. This could be a provocative statement, a surprising statistic, or a relatable anecdote that establishes the stakes and draws your audience in.

As you move into the body of your presentation, escalate the "action" by introducing new information, increasing the stakes, or revealing significant facts that build towards a climax. Use storytelling techniques like cliffhangers, plot twists, and dramatic reveals to keep your audience on the edge of their seats, wondering what will happen next.

Following this, your conclusion should serve as the resolution, answering the initial questions posed or summarizing the journey in a satisfying and complete way. Use callback humor (a comedic technique where a joke or reference made earlier in a performance or conversation is brought back unexpectedly later on, often in a new context. This creates humor through repetition and surprise.)

Here's an example I might use: "Many speakers worry about forgetting their material. One common advice is to imagine the audience in their underwear to feel less intimidated. However, this can backfire if you start giggling at the thought of your CEO in boxer shorts with heart patterns." Then, later in my presentation, when discussing visual aids, I may say: "When preparing slides, remember that less is more. You want your audience focused on your words, not squinting at a cluttered screen. After all, you're not trying to distract them from imagining you in your underwear – that's supposed to be your trick, remember?"

Incorporate a Full Circle Ending. This is a storytelling technique where the conclusion of a narrative returns to an element, theme, or idea introduced at the beginning. This creates a sense of completeness and symmetry, often leaving the audience with a satisfying feeling of closure. Here's an example of a Full Circle Ending for a speech about overcoming challenges in the workplace:

Opening: "Ladies and gentlemen, when I entered my first job 20 years ago, I was carrying a briefcase my father had given me. He said, 'This briefcase is empty now, but by the time you retire, it should be full of experience, wisdom, and stories.'" [The speaker then discusses various challenges faced in their career and the lessons learned from each.] Closing: "As I stand here today, I realize that briefcase my father gave me isn't just full – it's overflowing. Every challenge we face in our professional lives is an opportunity to add something valuable to our briefcases. So, I encourage you to embrace the difficulties, learn from the setbacks, and fill your briefcase. Because at the end of the day, it's not about what you carry – it's about the wisdom you've gained along the way."

Full-circle endings or powerful quotes are great ways to create a sense of closure and reinforce your main message.

Include Conflict and Resolution

Introducing conflict or challenge in your story provides tension that can pique and sustain interest. The conflict could be a market challenge your company faces, a common misconception about your field, or a problem your product or service can solve. By presenting this conflict and guiding your audience through the steps toward resolution, you mimic the emotional satisfaction of a story, resolving its plot. The resolution should provide a clear answer or solution, ideally tied to the action you want your audience to take. For example, if you're presenting a new marketing strategy, you might introduce the conflict by discussing the declining effectiveness of traditional advertising methods. You could share statistics about ad fatigue, banner blindness, and the rise of ad-blocking software, painting a picture of the challenges marketers face in reaching their target audiences.

As you move into the body of your presentation, you could introduce your new marketing strategy as the solution to this conflict. Use case studies, examples, and data to show how your approach addresses your outlined problems and delivers better results than traditional methods. Build a sense of excitement and possibility around your solution, helping your audience envision a future where this conflict is resolved.

In your conclusion, you could offer a clear call to action that ties your solution to your audience's needs and goals. For example, you might invite them to attend a workshop, sign up for a free trial, or collaborate with your team to implement the new strategy in their organization. Providing a clear path forward and a sense of resolution leaves your audience empowered and motivated to take action.

Personal Stories vs. Universal Themes

Balancing personal stories with universal themes can significantly enhance the relatability of your presentation. Personal stories allow your audience to see real-world applications of your points and make your presentation more engaging. However, tying these examples to universal themes—such as success, innovation, perseverance, or collaboration—elevates your narrative, connecting individual stories to broader, more relatable contexts. This blend makes your presentation more impactful and ensures it resonates with a diverse audience. For example, if you're giving a presentation about leadership, you might share a personal story about a difficult decision you made as a manager. You may have to choose between two equally qualified candidates for a promotion or navigate a tense conflict between team members. By sharing the specifics of your own experience, you give your audience a window into the realities of leadership and the challenges that come with it.

On the other hand, you could tie your story to universal themes like integrity, fairness, or empathy to make it more broadly applicable. You could discuss how your decision-making process was guided by a commitment to doing what was right, even when it was difficult. Or you could highlight how your ability to see the situation from multiple perspectives and consider the needs of all parties involved helped you find a resolution that worked for everyone. Connecting your personal story to these universal themes makes it more relatable to audience members who may not have had the same experience but can still identify with the underlying principles and emotions. You also elevate your story from a simple anecdote to a powerful illustration of larger truths about leadership, teamwork, and human nature.

Balancing specificity and universality is essential when incorporating personal stories into your presentations. Share enough detail to make your story vivid and engaging, but also take the time to draw out the broader lessons and themes that make it relevant to your audience. Doing so creates an authentic and inclusive narrative, inviting your audience to see themselves in your experiences and apply your insights to their lives and work.

Framework for Inspirational Speeches

The Hero's Journey is a robust narrative framework that has shaped stories from ancient myths to modern cinema. It was recognized and coined by literature professor Joseph Campbell, who noticed all stories and myths followed a distinct pattern and he broke it down into twelve sections. Its universal appeal lies in the journey of a hero who ventures from the ordinary into the extraordinary, faces challenges, secures victory, and returns transformed. This framework is incredibly effective in public speaking, especially when crafting speeches that aim to inspire and motivate.

Understanding the Hero's Journey in the context of public speaking involves recognizing each part of the journey and how it can mirror the path you want your audience to embark upon:

1. The Ordinary World: the hero's everyday life before the adventure begins. In a presentation, this is where you introduce the status quo that your audience is familiar with. You might discuss your audience's challenges or limitations in their current situation, setting the stage for the journey ahead.

2. The Call to Adventure: the hero is presented with a problem, challenge, or opportunity. In your presentation, this is where you introduce the central theme or idea that will be the focus of your talk. You might present a new perspective, a groundbreaking solution, or a call to action that challenges your audience to step out of their comfort zone.

3. Refusal of the Call: the hero hesitates to accept the challenge due to fear, insecurity, or inadequacy. In your presentation, acknowledge the doubts or concerns that your audience might have about embarking on this journey. Address their fears and provide reassurance that the journey is worth taking.

4. Meeting the Mentor: the hero encounters a mentor who provides guidance, training, or gifts to help them overcome their fears and accept the call. In your presentation, you can position yourself as the mentor, offering expertise, insights, and support to guide your audience through the challenges ahead.

5. Crossing the Threshold: the hero commits to the adventure and enters the particular world. In your presentation, this is where you invite your audience to fully engage with your ideas and take the first steps towards change. You might offer a specific tool, strategy, or mindset shift that helps them cross the threshold into a new way of thinking or being.

6. Tests, Allies, and Enemies: the hero faces challenges, makes allies, and confronts enemies. In your presentation, discuss the obstacles and setbacks that your audience might face on their journey. Share examples of how others have navigated similar challenges and the lessons they learned. Highlight the importance of building a support network and surrounding oneself with positive influences.

7. Approach to the Inmost Cave: the hero approaches the central ordeal of the adventure. In your presentation, build suspense and anticipation for the main point or revelation that will be the turning point of your talk. Foreshadow the challenges and rewards that await your audience as they near the heart of their journey.

8. The Ordeal: the hero faces the most significant challenge and experiences "death" (literal or metaphorical). In your presentation, this is where you confront the most critical obstacle or fear that holds your audience back. You might share a personal story of facing a similar challenge and its transformative impact on your life. Emphasize the importance of perseverance and growth from pushing through difficult times.

9. Reward: the hero survives and gains the reward (knowledge, treasure, or insight). In your presentation, celebrate the breakthroughs and victories that your audience will experience as they overcome their challenges. Share the benefits and opportunities that await them on the other side of their journey.

10. The Road Back: the hero returns to the ordinary world. In your presentation, acknowledge that the journey is not over and that there will be ongoing challenges and opportunities for growth. Encourage your audience to integrate their newfound knowledge and insights into their daily lives and to continue pushing forward.

11. Resurrection: the hero faces a final test where the knowledge or treasure gained is put to use. In your presentation, offer a final call to action or challenge that allows your audience to apply what they've learned. Encourage them to take concrete steps towards their goals and force positive change in their lives and communities.

12. Return with the Elixir: the hero returns to the ordinary world with a reward or knowledge that can benefit others. In your presentation, emphasize the ripple effect your audience's journey will have on those around them. Inspire them to share their insights and experiences with others and to be catalysts for transformation in their spheres of influence.

By structuring your presentation around the Hero's Journey framework, you create a powerful narrative that resonates with your audience profoundly and emotionally.

Identifying with the Audience

Position your audience as the story's hero to make your speech impactful. Speak directly to their experiences, challenges, and aspirations. Use second-person narrative or direct questions to make your speech more engaging and personal. This technique increases engagement and encourages personal reflection, creating a deeper emotional connection with your message. For example, instead of saying, "Many people struggle with public speaking anxiety," you could say, "Have you ever felt your heart race and your palms sweat at the thought of giving a presentation? You're not alone." By using "you" language and inviting your audience to reflect on their own experiences, you create a sense of empathy and connection that makes your message feel more relevant and applicable.

Similarly, instead of saying, "Effective leaders need to communicate their vision clearly," you could say, "Imagine yourself as a leader, inspiring your team to achieve greatness. How will you communicate your vision to motivate and empower them?" By placing your audience in the protagonist role and inviting them to envision themselves in the situation you're describing, you make your message more engaging and memorable.

Throughout your presentation, look for opportunities to highlight how your audience can relate to the hero's journey. Emphasize the universal themes and emotions your story touches on, such as the desire for growth, the fear of failure, or the satisfaction of overcoming obstacles. Use inclusive language that makes your audience feel seen and understood, such as "we" instead of "I."

By positioning your audience as the story's hero and speaking directly to their experiences and aspirations, you create a powerful sense of identification that makes your message more impactful and inspiring. Your audience will feel like you are speaking directly to them, understanding their challenges, and rooting for their success. They will be more likely to see themselves in your story and feel motivated to take action based on your message.

Balancing Emotion and Logic

To achieve a balance between emotional and logical appeals, it's essential to understand that emotions can significantly influence how information is perceived and retained. Emotional appeals connect with the audience on a human level, making your message more relatable and memorable. However, these appeals must be grounded in logical facts to maintain credibility and substance. Begin by identifying the core message of your presentation and the logical data that supports it, then weave in emotional elements that complement this data. For example, if you're giving a presentation about the importance of employee well-being in the workplace, you could start with some statistics about the impact of stress and burnout on productivity, absenteeism, and turnover. These logical data points establish the scope and severity of the problem, appealing to your audience's rational side.

To make your message more emotionally resonant, you could follow up the data with a personal story about an employee who struggled with work-life balance and the toll it took on their health and happiness. By putting a human face on the issue and describing the emotional impact of poor well-being, you create a sense of empathy and connection that makes your message feel more urgent and relevant.

Similarly, if you're giving a presentation about the benefits of a new product or service, you could start with some logical data points about its features, performance, and ROI. These appeals to reason and evidence help to establish the credibility and value of your offering. To make your message more emotionally compelling, you could share a customer success story that highlights the real-world impact of your product or service. By describing how your offering helped a specific customer overcome a challenge or achieve a goal, you create a sense of aspiration and possibility that makes your message more inspiring and memorable.

The key to balancing emotional and logical appeals is to use them in a complementary and mutually reinforcing way. Logical appeals provide the foundation and credibility for your message, while emotional appeals make it more relatable and inspiring. By weaving these two types of appeals together throughout your presentation, you create a more well-rounded and persuasive argument that engages your audience's head and heart.

Common Pitfalls to Avoid

While storytelling is a powerful tool in public speaking, there are some common pitfalls to avoid:

1. Overusing Personal Anecdotes: while personal stories can be engaging, too many can make your presentation feel self-indulgent or disconnected from your main message.

2. Failing to Tie Stories to the Core Message: every story you include should have a clear purpose and contribute to your overall message.

3. Neglecting the Emotional Arc: avoid flat or disjointed stories that fail to create an emotional connection or provide a clear takeaway.

4. Overlooking the Importance of Practice: storytelling requires practice and refinement to be effective.

5. Relying Too Heavily on Storytelling: stories are powerful, but they should be balanced with other presentation elements, such as data, evidence, and logical arguments.

6. Failing to Consider the Audience: not all stories will resonate with all audiences.

7. Overcomplicating the Story: a good story should be clear, concise, and easy to follow.

8. Neglecting the Power of Visuals: stories are often more powerful when accompanied by visual aids that help bring the narrative to life.

By being aware of and avoiding these common pitfalls, you can effectively incorporate storytelling into your presentations to enhance your credibility, engage your audience, and drive your message home.

Storytelling is a transformative skill for you as a public speaker. As you can see, it offers a powerful way to connect with audiences on multiple levels. It is more than mere entertainment; it is a universal language that brings complex ideas to life and creates deep emotional resonance. You can create informative, profoundly engaging, and memorable presentations by skillfully blending emotional appeals with logical arguments. Ultimately, the art of storytelling is about more than just relaying information; it's about creating a shared experience that moves, inspires, and motivates.

Storytelling is an essential tool that should be in every public speaker's kit.

6

Body Language and Nonverbal Communication

"The most important thing in communication is to hear what isn't being said." P Drucker

Mastering the art of body language in public speaking is like learning to play a complex musical instrument. It requires understanding the basics, continuous practice, and, most importantly, a keen sense of awareness and adaptability. Appreciating the subtle yet powerful nonverbal language cues can transform your ability to persuade, command respect, and convey confidence in public speaking.

This chapter is dedicated to unraveling the complexities of body language and promoting you to a communicator who speaks not only with words but with every nuance of your being.

Understanding Nonverbal Signals

Body language is a form of nonverbal communication that includes facial expressions, gestures, posture, and physical distance.

At the core of mastering body language is understanding that your body speaks a language as intricate as any spoken dialect. Nonverbal cues can affirm or contradict what's being said, reveal emotions not explicitly expressed, and enhance or undermine the perceived sincerity of your message. For instance, crossing your arms while delivering a message intended to welcome feedback can subconsciously signal defensiveness, deterring the engagement you seek.

Your words alone are just a fraction of what your audience is absorbing. How you carry yourself, your facial expressions, and your physical presence can reinforce or undermine the verbal content you're delivering.

Your body language should complement and reinforce your verbal message, not contradict it. Congruence between what you're saying and how you're saying it is vital for building trust and credibility with your audience. For example, suppose you verbally express enthusiasm or passion about a topic. In that case, your body language should reflect that energy through open gestures, an animated presence, and facial expressions that convey genuine excitement. Conversely, if you deliver a somber or severe message, your body language should match that tone with a more subdued, grounded demeanor.

Nonverbal signals can broadly be categorized into positive and negative cues, each capable of creating vastly different reactions from your audience. Positive body language includes maintaining an open posture, nodding, smiling, and using hand gestures that indicate openness and inclusiveness. These cues make you, the speaker, appear approachable, engaged, and confident. Conversely, negative body language, such as avoiding eye contact, fidgeting, or maintaining a closed posture (like crossed arms or legs), can make a speaker seem untrustworthy, disinterested, or even nervous.

Facial Expressions

Facial expressions are one of the most important aspects of nonverbal communication, as they convey various emotions and attitudes. Key facial expressions to be aware of include:

1. Smiling: a genuine smile can help create a positive, approachable demeanor and build rapport with the audience.

2. Frowning: depending on the context, frowning can convey disapproval, concern, or concentration.

3. Raised eyebrows: raised eyebrows can indicate surprise, interest, or skepticism.

4. Narrowed eyes: narrowed eyes can suggest suspicion, anger, or intense focus.

To use facial expressions effectively, maintain a natural, congruent expression that aligns with your verbal message and stay relaxed.

Practicing Awareness

Developing an awareness of your body language is an essential first step. Begin by observing how you communicate in business settings and everyday interactions. Consider questions like:

How do you react when faced with questions? Do you look puzzled or confronted?

What does your posture say about your level of interest in a conversation? Are you leaning in to listen or sitting back looking at your watch?

A practical exercise to enhance awareness is to ask someone to watch you and give honest feedback or record yourself presenting and look for inconsistencies between your verbal and nonverbal cues. For example, are you saying "yes" while shaking your head from side to side? Such mismatches can confuse your audience and detract from your message's credibility. Gradually, you will start to notice patterns and can correct them.

Using Gestures to Enhance Your Message

Gestures are potent tools for emphasizing your message. When used deliberately, they can significantly strengthen the delivery of your message, making it more memorable and engaging for your audience. However, it's essential to avoid excessive, aimless gesturing, which can be distracting and undermine your professionalism. Gestures should feel natural and purposeful, almost like visual punctuation for your words.

One effective strategy is to practice incorporating gestures that directly illustrate or emphasize key points in your speech—for example, using hand motions to represent size, height, or numerical values when stating facts and figures or opening your arms wide when expressing an overarching concept or idea. Keep all gestures authentic; they must feel natural and confident, not forced or overdone.

Different types of gestures can convey different meanings and emotional undertones. They can be categorized into descriptive, emotive, suggestive, and prompting gestures:

1. Descriptive gestures describe or mimic physical details about an object or action, such as the size or shape of something.

2. Emotive gestures express feelings like joy or frustration.

3. Suggestive gestures subtly hint at or suggest an idea, often used to provoke thought or highlight implications.

4. Prompting gestures are intended to elicit a response from the audience, such as raising your hand to signal them to stop or think.

Understanding these varieties and their associated meanings allows you to use gestures more effectively to complement your verbal messages. For instance, when trying to convey the importance of a concept, you might clench your fist to communicate intensity and conviction visually.

When speaking to diverse or international audiences, it's crucial to consider how cultural differences can influence the interpretation of your gestures. What might be a positive gesture in one culture could be offensive or confusing in another. For example, the thumbs-up gesture is considered affirmative in many Western cultures but can be offensive in parts of the Middle East and South America. Similarly, pointing one finger is often rude in Asian and African cultures, where pointing with an open hand is preferable. If you need more clarification, observe the gestures used by local speakers and adapt accordingly.

Eye Contact and Building Trust

Eye contact is a fundamental component of communication that can bridge the gap between speaker and listener, fostering a connection of trust and understanding. The eyes, often described as the windows to the soul, can convey honesty, confidence, and empathy—qualities essential for effective communication.

In public speaking, consistent eye contact helps hold the audience's attention and convey confidence in the subject matter. It also plays a critical role in making your delivery appear sincere and genuine, bolstering the audience's trust in you and your message. When you look someone in the eyes, you say, "I am open to communication, and I value this interaction." This nonverbal cue is crucial in making your audience feel acknowledged and respected.

Effective eye contact goes beyond merely 'looking' at your audience. It involves intentionally connecting with your listeners through your gaze, which should be inviting and informative. Eye contact can guide your audience through your presentation, emphasizing key points and facilitating a better understanding of your message. When executed well, it helps to create an atmosphere of inclusivity and engagement, making each audience member feel as though you are speaking directly to them, thus enhancing the overall impact of your speech.

Understanding the balance between too much and too little eye contact is essential. Excessive eye contact can be perceived as intimidating or aggressive, which may cause discomfort or disengage your audience. On the other hand, insufficient eye contact can be interpreted as a lack of confidence, interest, or sincerity, potentially undermining your credibility and the trust you wish to establish.

Finding the right balance involves maintaining eye contact long enough to connect with the audience, typically around three to five seconds per person or group, before shifting your gaze naturally to others in the audience. This balance is about the duration and the distribution of your eye contact across the audience.

Ensure that your eye contact is evenly distributed to include everyone in the conversation, regardless of their position. Neglecting certain areas or individuals can lead to feelings of exclusion and reduce your audience's overall engagement. Consider implementing one of the following strategic techniques:

1. The 'lighthouse' technique: sweep your gaze across the audience in a slow, steady motion, like a lighthouse beam. This technique ensures that your attention reaches everyone, creating a sense of engagement and connection throughout the room.

2. The 'triangular gazing' method: this involves making eye contact with three different people in various parts of the audience at random intervals. This method can make your gaze feel more natural and spontaneous while covering a broad range of the audience space.

Practice focusing on the eyes of your audience members during rehearsals or when speaking to smaller groups. This practice will help you become more comfortable maintaining eye contact in less formal settings, building your confidence and proficiency over time. It is also helpful to simulate eye contact when practicing alone by using placeholders like chairs or objects to represent different audience members, training yourself to make natural transitions between focal points.

Overcoming Eye Contact Anxiety

For many, maintaining eye contact during a presentation can evoke anxiety stemming from the vulnerability of being in the spotlight.

To overcome this anxiety, start by understanding that eye contact is a skill that improves with practice and exposure. Begin in low-pressure situations, such as conversations with friends or during team meetings, and gradually work your way up to larger, more formal settings.

This gradual exposure can help desensitize your apprehensions, making eye contact feel more natural and less daunting.

Another technique is to focus on the friendly faces in the audience—the individuals who nod, smile, or otherwise positively engage with your presentation. Focusing on these receptive audience members can boost your confidence and reduce anxiety, making maintaining eye contact with the rest of the room easier.

Remember that your audience generally wants you to succeed, and their gaze often reflects interest and encouragement rather than judgment.

The Power of Pausing

Strategic pauses in public speaking are not mere breaks in sound; they are purposeful tools that help to emphasize points, give the audience time to absorb information, and create an element of suspense or anticipation. Imagine delivering a powerful statement and then pausing—this silence allows your words to resonate, giving the audience time to reflect on their significance. This technique can transform a good speech into an unforgettable one by punctuating your message with moments that invite the audience into more profound thought or heightened emotion.

The timing and length of pauses are crucial for achieving the desired effect without disrupting the flow of your speech. Generally, a pause can range from a half-second to up to four seconds, depending on its purpose. Shorter pauses are effective for slight emphasis and allow the audience to catch up with quick shifts in the topic. Longer pauses help draw attention to significant transitions or conclusions within your speech. They can also be instrumental when you switch from one section of your presentation to another, signaling a shift in focus or introducing a new concept.

To master pauses, consider the rhythm of your speech and the nature of your content. For instance, after introducing a controversial or surprising statistic, a longer pause can allow the magnitude of the information to sink in. Conversely, when listing several points quickly, shorter pauses can help maintain the momentum of the speech while still marking each item.

The key is to balance pauses with the natural cadence of your speech, ensuring they enhance rather than disrupt your delivery.

Practicing the use of pauses can dramatically improve the effectiveness of your speech. Identify spots in your remarks where a pause could enhance understanding or emphasize a point. During rehearsals, experiment with different lengths of pauses to see how they affect the delivery and reception of your message.

Recording your practice sessions can be beneficial. Playback allows you to objectively assess the timing and impact of your pauses and make adjustments as needed. Over time, you will develop a sense of when and how to use pauses most effectively to complement your speaking style and message.

Another helpful practice is reading passages from books or speeches aloud, paying attention to punctuation like commas, periods, and paragraph breaks, and using them as cues for natural pauses. This exercise can help you get accustomed to the rhythmic use of pauses in language.

You can also practice with a partner or coach who can provide feedback on the timing and effectiveness of your pauses, offering insights you might not notice on your own.

Embracing the Sound of Silence

Overcoming the fear of silence is essential for using pauses effectively. Many speakers fear that moments of silence may be perceived as awkward or a sign of forgetfulness. However, when used deliberately, silence is a powerful tool that shows confidence and control.

To overcome this fear, start by incorporating brief pauses into your speeches, gradually increasing their duration as you become more comfortable with the silence. Remind yourself that these pauses are not empty spaces but opportunities for your message to be absorbed and understood more deeply by your audience.

By understanding the strategic use of pauses, you enhance the clarity and impact of your presentations and demonstrate professionalism and confidence that sets you apart as a speaker. As you continue to integrate effective pauses into your speeches, remember that silence, like speech, is a form of communication that, when used wisely, can transform the pace and perception of your public speaking endeavors.

Mastering the Use of Space on Stage

When you step onto a stage, you're not just delivering a speech but commanding a space. Your movement and positioning within that space can significantly influence how your message is perceived and received.

Spatial awareness in public speaking involves understanding how the physical space you occupy can either enhance or detract from the impact of your message. It's about arranging your movements to complement your words, creating a blend of verbal and visual communication that captivates your audience.

The concept of spatial awareness extends beyond simply not bumping into furniture or avoiding awkward stances. It encompasses strategically using your presence in the room to command attention and convey confidence. For instance, moving toward the audience can make your delivery feel more intimate and engaged, particularly when making key points. Conversely, stepping back can allow the audience to reflect or absorb the gravity of what you've just said.

This dynamic approach to using space can make your presentation feel like a well-choreographed performance rather than a static lecture, keeping the audience visually and mentally engaged.

Every step you take on stage should serve a purpose. Purposeful movement is about making your physical actions deliberate in your message delivery. For example, if you're discussing a journey or progression, physically moving from one side of the stage to the other can visually represent this concept, making it more tangible for your audience. Similarly, stepping forward when sharing personal anecdotes can create a feeling of closeness and authenticity. The key is to ensure that your movements align with and enhance your verbal message rather than seeming random or distracting.

Plan your space usage in advance to integrate purposeful movement into your presentations. Consider the key points of your presentation and how movement could underscore these moments. During rehearsals, mark the spots on the stage where you plan to stand or move during different speech segments. This preparation helps you move confidently and fluidly, avoiding unnecessary or awkward transitions that can disrupt your delivery flow.

Developing a commanding stage presence is an essential part of effective public speaking. It's about projecting confidence and authority through your posture, movements, and how you occupy the space. A vital stage presence reassures the audience of your expertise and credibility, making your message more persuasive.

To cultivate a powerful stage presence, start by practicing your posture. Stand straight, with shoulders back and head held high, projecting confidence and readiness. Practice your movements to ensure they are smooth and purposeful. Use video recordings to critique your performance and make adjustments where necessary. If you can, practice in the venue where you will speak. Familiarity with the exact space can boost your confidence and help you tailor your movements and positioning to the specific stage and audience layout.

The Impact of Dress and Appearance

When you step onto the stage, the first thing your audience perceives, even before you utter a word, is your appearance. This initial visual impression can significantly influence how your message is received and establish or erode your credibility within seconds.

'Dressing for success' in public speaking is not about superficial aesthetics but strategically using your wardrobe to complement your message. It involves choosing attire that enhances your comfort and confidence and aligns with your audience's expectations and norms.

Understanding the subtle dynamics of audience expectations regarding professional appearance is crucial. For instance, dressing in a sharply tailored suit might be appropriate for a corporate finance conference, where traditional business attire can convey professionalism and competence. Conversely, suppose you are addressing a tech start-up event. In that case, a more casual blazer and jeans might be more relatable, aligning with that audience's innovative and laid-back culture. The key is to research and understand your audience's professional norms beforehand. This preparatory step ensures that your appearance supports your speech, reinforcing your key messages rather than distracting from them.

I talk more about this topic in Chapter 12 under the banner of building your brand.

I've created a short checklist to help you remember the most critical points of non-verbal communication when presenting.

Body Language Checklist for Public Speakers

1. Open body language: avoid crossing arms or creating barriers between you and the audience to appear more approachable and confident.

2. Posture: stand tall with shoulders back and chin up to project confidence and command attention.

3. Stance: keep your feet shoulder-width apart for a stable, grounded appearance.

4. Facial expressions: ensure your facial expressions match your message and convey appropriate emotions.

5. Hand gestures: use purposeful, open gestures to emphasize points and appear more engaging.

6. Pause: use strategic pauses to emphasize points, allow audience reflection, and control pacing.

7. Silence: remember to see silence as an opportunity for your message to be absorbed and understood more deeply by your audience.

8. Proximity: be aware of your distance from the audience and adjust for intimacy or authority as needed.

9. Stage movement: move purposefully on stage to maintain audience engagement and emphasize key points.

10. Dress For Success: make sure your outfit aligns with the expectations of your audience.

As you practice these techniques, your confidence and connection with audiences will strengthen, and your overall effectiveness as a speaker will grow. Remember that mastering these skills is a journey of self-discovery and continuous improvement that takes time.

Every great speaker you admire has honed these skills through practice and persistence. You, too, have the power to command the stage, so step forward with confidence, knowing that with each presentation, you're not just speaking – you're communicating with your entire being.

Let your body language amplify your voice in ways words alone never could.

7

Vocal Techniques for Maximum Impact

"Your voice is your calling card." S Rye

When used effectively, the human voice is a powerful instrument that can captivate, persuade, and inspire an audience. As a public speaker, your vocal delivery is crucial in engaging listeners and conveying your message. However, many speakers fall into the trap of delivering their speeches in a monotonous, flat tone that fails to capture the attention or emotions of their audience. This is where vocal variety comes in – the art of using changes in pitch, volume, pace, and tone to add depth, meaning, and interest to your words.

This chapter explores the importance of vocal variety in public speaking, and I share practical exercises and techniques to help you develop your vocal skills. We will also look at the speeches of renowned speakers to understand how they use vocal variety to enhance their delivery. In addition, I share strategies for incorporating vocal variety into your presentations, ensuring you keep your audience engaged and attentive throughout your speech.

The Power of Vocal Variety

Imagine listening to a speaker maintaining the same volume, pitch, and pace throughout their presentation. No matter how compelling their message or how well-crafted their words are, the lack of vocal variety will likely leave you feeling bored, disengaged, or even frustrated.

On the other hand, a speaker who skillfully employs vocal variety can transform even the most complex or dry topics into a captivating and memorable experience for their audience.

Vocal variety serves several vital functions in public speaking:

1. Maintaining audience attention: by varying your vocal delivery, you create a dynamic and engaging experience that keeps your listeners focused and interested in your message. Monotony is the enemy of attention, and vocal variety is the antidote.

2. Conveying emotions and meaning: your voice can convey a wide range of emotions, from passion and excitement to sincerity and concern. By aligning your vocal delivery with the emotional content of your words, you can create a deeper connection with your audience and enhance the impact of your message.

3. Emphasizing key points: strategic changes in volume, pitch, or pace can help highlight the essential ideas in your speech, ensuring that your audience gets all the crucial takeaways. This is particularly important when delivering complex or information-dense content.

4. Creating a conversational tone: incorporating vocal variety can help you sound more natural, conversational, and relatable to your audience, even in formal speaking contexts. This conversational approach can break down barriers between the speaker and the audience, fostering a sense of connection and trust.

Developing Your Vocal Variety

Like any skill, developing vocal variety takes practice and intentional effort. Here are some exercises and techniques you can use to expand your vocal range and expressiveness:

Diaphragmatic breathing: proper breathing is the foundation of a robust and flexible voice. Practice taking deep breaths from your diaphragm, filling your lungs, and exhaling slowly and evenly. This will help you project your voice without straining and give you greater control over your vocal delivery. Inadequate breathing can lead to a weak, strained, or monotonous voice, quickly losing your audience's attention. A speaker who takes shallow breaths from the chest causes their voice to sound thin and weak.

In contrast, a speaker who breathes deeply from their diaphragm allows their voice to resonate with fullness and power, making a significant difference in vocal impact. To practice diaphragmatic breathing, place one hand on your chest and the other on your belly. Breathe deeply through your nose, focusing on expanding your belly rather than your chest. Exhale slowly through your mouth, feeling your belly contract. Repeat this process several times, ensuring your chest remains relatively still while your belly rises and falls.

Exploring volume: volume refers to the loudness or softness of your voice. Varying your volume can help emphasize important points, create contrast, and maintain your audience's attention. A louder volume can convey excitement, passion, or urgency, while a softer volume can suggest intimacy, sincerity, or confidentiality. Practice speaking at different volumes, from a whisper to a loud projected voice. Be sure to maintain good breath support and avoid shouting or straining your voice.

A great exercise is to choose a simple phrase, such as "I have something important to say," and repeat it at different volume levels, from a whisper to a normal speaking voice to a loud, projected voice. Notice how the volume change affects the words' perceived meaning and impact. When incorporating volume changes into your speeches, be strategic and intentional. Use louder volumes sparingly, reserving them for your presentation's most critical or exciting points. This contrast will make those moments stand out and grab your audience's attention. Conversely, a softer volume can draw your listeners in, creating a sense of intimacy and encouraging them to focus more intently on your words.

Playing with pitch: pitch refers to the highness or lowness of your voice. Varying your pitch can help emphasize key points, create differences, and maintain your audience's attention. A higher pitch can convey excitement or urgency, while a lower pitch can suggest authority or seriousness. A speaker may use a higher pitch when sharing a surprising or exciting statistic, drawing their audience's attention to the significance of the information. Conversely, they may lower their pitch to convey gravity and importance when delivering a serious or somber message.

To increase your pitch range, try speaking or singing a phrase starting at your lowest comfortable pitch and gradually ascending to your highest comfortable pitch, then back down again. You can also practice sliding your voice up and down in a siren-like motion to help loosen and stretch your vocal cords. You can create a more dynamic and engaging delivery by strategically varying your pitch throughout your speech.

Pacing for impact: the pace at which you speak can significantly impact the effectiveness of your message. Speaking too quickly can overwhelm your audience and make it difficult for them to process your ideas. On the other hand, speaking too slowly can cause your listeners to lose interest or become impatient.

To practice pacing, try reading a passage from a book or article at different speeds, from very slow to very fast. Notice how the change in pace affects the meaning and emotional impact of the words. Aim for a conversational pace that allows your audience to follow and comprehend your message while maintaining momentum easily. Consider your message's complexity and emotional content when incorporating pacing changes into your speeches. When introducing a new or elaborate idea, slow down your pace to give your audience time to absorb and process the information. When sharing a humorous anecdote or an exciting story, slightly increase your pace to build energy and engagement. Remember to use pauses strategically to emphasize critical points, allow for audience reactions, or create dramatic tension. A well-timed pause can be just as powerful as a well-chosen word.

Varying your vocal tone: vocal tone refers to your voice's emotional quality and character, such as warmth, enthusiasm, or sincerity. Varying your tone can help convey the appropriate emotion, build a connection with your audience, and enhance the impact of your message.

To practice vocal tone, try delivering the exact phrase or sentence with different emotional inflections, such as happiness, sadness, anger, or surprise. Notice how the tone change affects the words' assumed meaning and impact. You can also practice mimicking the vocal tones of various speakers or characters to expand your range and flexibility. Be authentic and congruent with your message when incorporating vocal tone changes into your speeches. If you're sharing a personal story, use a warm, sincere tone to build a connection with your audience. If you deliver a call to action, use an enthusiastic, passionate tone to inspire and motivate your listeners.

Articulation in Speech

In addition to vocal variety, articulation is another critical component of effective vocal delivery. Articulation refers to the clarity and precision with which you pronounce words and phrases, ensuring your audience quickly understands your message. Poor articulation can result in mumbled, slurred, or rushed speech, which can be difficult for your audience to follow and comprehend. This can lead to frustration, disengagement, and even misinterpreting your message.

To improve your articulation, practice the following techniques:

1. Enunciation: focus on pronouncing each syllable and word clearly and distinctly, particularly at the beginning and end of words. Pay special attention to consonant sounds, which can often become muddled or dropped in casual speech.

2. Tongue twisters: practice saying tongue twisters, such as "She sells seashells by the seashore" or "Peter Piper picked a peck of pickled peppers." These exercises can help improve the agility and precision of your tongue and lips, leading to more accurate articulation.

3. Slow down: aim for a slightly slower pace than your average conversational speed when speaking. This will give you more time to articulate each word and phrase clearly without rushing or mumbling. Remember, a slower pace can also convey a sense of authority and importance. But too slow can be tedious—it's a fine line, but not as tricky as it sounds. Record your rehearsals, and you'll immediately hear the difference.

Choosing Words that Resonate

Your chosen words can significantly impact how your audience receives and understands your message. When selecting the language for your speeches, consider the following:

1. Clarity and simplicity: use clear, concise language that is easily understood by your audience. Avoid jargon, technical terms, or overly complex vocabulary unless it is essential to your message and your audience is familiar with the terminology.

2. Vivid and descriptive language: use language that paints a picture in your audience's minds, engaging their senses and emotions. Incorporate metaphors, similes, and other descriptive techniques to make your message more memorable and impactful.

3. Inclusive language: be mindful of your audience's diversity and choose inclusive and respectful language of different backgrounds, experiences, and perspectives. Avoid language that is biased, stereotypical, or offensive.

4. Rhetorical devices: use rhetorical devices like repetition, alliteration, and parallel structure (see examples below) to make your language more engaging and memorable. These tools can help emphasize key points, create a sense of rhythm and flow, and make your message more persuasive.

Soundbites: Powerful Little Statements

Soundbites are concise, memorable phrases that encapsulate the essence of your message. These powerful statements are often quoted and shared long after your speech has ended, helping to extend the impact and reach of your ideas.

To craft compelling soundbites, consider the following tips:

1. Keep it concise: aim for short, punchy phrases that are easy to remember and repeat. Ideally, a soundbite should be 10-15 words.

2. Make it memorable: use descriptive language to evoke a sensory experience and vivid mental image in the listener's mind. Include metaphors to create deeper meaning, or use rhetorical techniques to make your soundbite stand out.

3. Tie it to your core message: ensure that your soundbite encapsulates your speech's key theme or takeaway, reinforcing the

main point you want your audience to remember.

4. Use parallel structure: craft your soundbite using parallel structure. For example, John F Kennedy said, "Ask not what your country can do for you; ask what you can do for your country." This technique creates a sense of balance and symmetry, making the phrase more memorable and impactful.

Analyzing Renowned Speakers

One of the best ways to learn about effective vocal delivery is to study the speeches of renowned speakers known for their powerful and engaging communication skills. By analyzing their use of vocal variety, articulation, language, and soundbites, you can gain valuable insights and inspiration for your speaking practice.

Michelle Obama: the former First Lady is a powerful speaker who uses vocal variety to convey authority, empathy, and conviction. Her speech at the 2020 Democratic National Convention showcased her ability to use pitch, pace, and tone changes to deliver a personal and political message. I encourage you to watch it and notice how she varies her pitch to emphasize key points and convey emotions.

For example, when she says, "You know I hate politics," her pitch lowers, signaling a sense of seriousness and personal conviction. She strategically slows down her pace when she wants to emphasize a point, such as when she says, "But let me be as honest and clear as I possibly can," drawing the audience's attention to her forthcoming message. Michelle Obama maintains a warm, conversational tone throughout her speech, creating a sense of connection with her audience. However, when discussing the gravity of the current political situation, her tone shifts to one of urgency and concern, underlining the importance of her message.

Greta Thunberg: the young climate activist has become known for her direct, impassioned speeches that call for urgent action on climate change. Her speech at the 2019 UN Climate Action Summit demonstrated her use of vocal variety to convey frustration, determination, and moral clarity. She uses volume to describe the intensity of her emotions and the urgency of her message. When she says, "How dare you," her volume increases, expressing her anger and frustration with world leaders' inaction on climate change.

Thunberg's pace is deliberate and measured, allowing her words to sink in and create a sense of gravity. She pauses strategically after powerful statements, such as "We are at the beginning of a mass extinction, and all you can talk about is money and fairy tales of eternal economic growth." Her tone is direct, unapologetic, and, at times, accusatory. This tone effectively conveys her sense of urgency and moral outrage, captivating her audience and demanding their attention.

Winston Churchill: known for his powerful oratory during World War II, Winston Churchill used various vocal techniques to inspire and motivate the British people. He varied his pitch and volume to emphasize critical points, used strategic pauses to create dramatic tension, and employed a rich, vibrant vocal tone to convey the gravity of the situation.

In his "We Shall Fight on the Beaches" speech, Churchill uses a wide range of pitch to convey the emotional weight of his words. When he says the words, "We shall fight on the beaches," his pitch lowers, creating a sense of determination and resolve. He varies his volume throughout the speech to emphasize key points and maintain engagement. He begins softly, drawing his audience in, and then gradually increases his volume to convey the crescendo of his message. Churchill's articulation is crisp and precise, ensuring that every word is clearly understood. This clarity adds to the power and impact of his message.

Martin Luther King Jr: King's "I Have a Dream" speech is a masterclass in vocal delivery. He used a powerful, rhythmic cadence to engage his audience, varied his pitch and volume to create a sense of urgency and passion, and employed repetition and parallel structure to make his message more memorable and impactful.

His tone is passionate, inspiring, and hopeful. He conveys a sense of moral authority and conviction that resonates with his audience and compels them to act. King strategically increases his volume to emphasize critical points and emotionally charged moments, such as when he says, "From every mountainside, let freedom ring," creating a powerful crescendo that stirs his audience.

While studying and learning from renowned speakers is essential, it is important to mention here that you shouldn't aim to copy someone else's style. Instead, incorporate vocal techniques that feel natural and authentic to your personality and communication style. View vocal variety as an opportunity to develop your speaking signature.

Incorporating Vocal Variety into Your Speeches

Now that you understand the importance of vocal variety and have explored techniques for developing your vocal skills, it's time to incorporate these principles into your speeches. Here are some strategies to help you integrate vocal variety into your preparation and delivery:

1. Script your vocal delivery: when crafting your speech, consider the words you'll say and how you'll say them. Make notes in your script to remind yourself of specific vocal techniques you want to use, such as pauses, volume changes, or tonal shifts.

2. Practice with intention: as you rehearse your speech, focus on incorporating vocal variety deliberately and intentionally. Experiment with different techniques and find what feels authentic and natural to your speaking style.

3. Record and review: record yourself delivering your speech and listen back critically. Identify areas where you can incorporate more vocal variety or improve your articulation and pacing. Adjust and continue practicing until you feel confident and comfortable with your delivery.

4. Seek feedback: ask a trusted colleague, friend, or mentor to listen to your speech and provide constructive feedback on your vocal delivery. They may notice patterns or areas for improvement that you've overlooked.

5. Warm up your voice: just as athletes warm up their muscles before a game, speakers should warm up their voices before a presentation. Spend a few minutes doing vocal exercises like humming, lip trills, or tongue twisters to loosen your vocal cords and prepare your voice for optimal performance. I've prepared a list of my favorite tongue twisters below.

Tongue Twisters for Speakers

1. "A blue-backed blackbird blew big bubbles." Concentrate on pronouncing each word separately.

2. "A monk's monkey mounted a monastery wall and munched melon and macaroni." Focus on the M sounds.

3. "Six sleek sharks swam swiftly in a spiral, chasing the shimmering schools of silvery sardines." This tongue twister relies heavily on rhythm; try to keep the flow smooth.

4. "Irish wristwatch. Swiss wristwatch." This one is a real challenge! Practice saying Irish and Swiss separately before combining them.

5. "A big black bug bit a big black bear, made the big black bear bleed blood." Focus on Bs and aim for clarity with each word.

6. "Knapsack straps. Knapsack straps. Knapsack straps." The difficulty is in the 'SK' sound at the end of 'knapsack' and the beginning of 'straps.' Practice them separately first.

7. "How many cookies could a good cook cook if a good cook could cook cookies?" Pay attention to the 'ook' sound.

8. "Supercalifragilisticexpialidocious." This single-word tongue twister is challenging to master. Break it down into more minor syllables and pronounce them individually before putting it all together.

Vocal variety is a powerful tool every public speaker should perfect to engage, persuade, and inspire their audience. By understanding the importance of pitch, volume, pace, tone, and articulation, plus practicing techniques to develop your vocal skills, you can unlock the full potential of your voice and become a more dynamic, confident, and effective communicator.

Remember, developing vocal variety is an ongoing process that requires intentional practice and self-reflection. By analyzing the speeches of renowned speakers, seeking feedback from others, and continually refining your vocal delivery, you can cultivate an authentic, engaging, and impactful speaking style.

So, the next time you step onto a stage or stand before an audience, tap into the power of your voice. Use it to paint vivid pictures, evoke powerful emotions, and leave a lasting impact on your listeners. Your words can change minds, inspire action, and transform lives.

Let your voice be the instrument that brings your message to life.

8

THE ART OF AUDIENCE ENGAGEMENT

"To sway an audience you must watch them as you speak." C K Wright

Public speaking is not always a smooth sailing experience. Even the most seasoned speakers encounter challenging situations that can disrupt the flow of their presentation and test their ability to maintain composure. These challenges can come in various forms, such as tough questions from the audience, interruptions during the speech, or dealing with complex listeners who may need to be more engaged.

Navigating these situations with poise and confidence is crucial for any public speaker. It requires thorough preparation, quick thinking, and adapting to the unexpected. This chapter explores strategies and techniques for handling these challenges, ensuring you can deliver your message effectively and maintain a positive rapport with all audience members.

Building Rapport

Before diving into specific strategies for dealing with challenging situations, it's essential to understand the importance of audience engagement and analysis. Engaging your audience is not just about delivering your content; it's about creating a meaningful connection with your listeners and understanding their needs, expectations, and potential reactions.

Building rapport with your audience is the foundation of effective communication. It involves creating a sense of trust, understanding, and shared purpose between you and your listeners. When you establish a genuine connection with your audience, they are more likely to be receptive to your message, even if you encounter challenges. To build rapport, demonstrate appreciation for your audience's presence and time. Acknowledge their effort in attending your presentation and emphasize the topic's importance for everyone involved. This shows respect and sets a positive tone for the rest of your speech.

Another great rapport-building tool is mirroring your audience's mood and energy level. This doesn't mean mimicking their behavior but rather attuning yourself to the general atmosphere in the room. If the audience seems severe and focused, adopt a similarly serious tone. Feel free to incorporate some light-hearted moments into your delivery if they appear more relaxed and open to humor. By matching your audience's energy, you will create a sense of alignment and connection.

Active listening is a crucial component of building rapport with your audience. Consider their questions and comments during Q&A sessions or when interacting with them. Respond thoughtfully and directly, showing that you value their input and are engaged in a genuine dialogue. This level of attentiveness demonstrates your respect for your audience and helps foster a more open and collaborative atmosphere.

Empathy plays a vital role in establishing an authentic connection. Put yourself in your audience's shoes and try to understand their perspectives, concerns, and aspirations related to your topic. Expressing empathy by acknowledging shared challenges or highlighting common goals creates a deeper resonance with your listeners. This emotional connection builds trust and encourages a more receptive and engaged audience.

Audience Analysis

Understanding your audience deeply is crucial to engaging them and navigating potential challenges effectively. I highly recommend conducting an audience analysis, including demographics and psychographics.

Demographics refer to the statistical characteristics of your audience, such as age, gender, education level, cultural background, and professional roles. Understanding these factors allows you to tailor your language, examples, and references to better resonate with your listeners. For instance, if you're addressing a predominantly younger audience, you might incorporate more contemporary cultural references and technological examples. On the other hand, if your audience consists mainly of experienced professionals, use more industry-specific terminology and draw upon historical examples relevant to their field. To gather demographic information, consider using pre-event surveys or researching the typical attendees of similar events.

While demographics provide a broad outline of your audience, psychographics delve deeper into their attitudes, values, interests, and motivations. Understanding your audience's psychographic profile allows you to connect with them more personally and emotionally. For example, if your audience values sustainability and environmental responsibility, you can emphasize the eco-friendly aspects of your topic and highlight how your ideas align with their values. Similarly, suppose your listeners are motivated by professional development and career advancement; you can focus on the practical applications of your message and how it can help them achieve their goals.

In addition to understanding your audience's demographics and psychographics, it's important to anticipate their needs and expectations. What do they hope to gain from your presentation? What questions or concerns might they have? By proactively addressing these issues, you demonstrate your preparedness and commitment to providing value to them.

Adapting on the Fly

Despite thorough preparation and audience analysis, there may be times when you need to adapt your presentation in real time based on audience feedback and reactions. This ability to be flexible and responsive is a hallmark of effective public speaking.

Pay close attention to your audience's verbal and nonverbal cues during your presentation. Are they nodding in agreement, or do they seem confused? Are they leaning forward with interest, or are they disengaged and distracted? These cues can help you gauge how well your message is being received and whether you need to make any adjustments.

If you notice signs of confusion or disengagement, consider the following strategies:

1. Pause and clarify: if you sense that a particular point may have been unclear, take a moment to rephrase or provide additional examples to help your audience better understand.

2. Engage in dialogue: encourage your audience to ask questions or share their thoughts. This can help you identify areas where you may need to provide more information or address specific concerns.

3. Adjust your pacing: if your audience seems overwhelmed or struggling to keep up, slow down your delivery and allow more time for them to process the information. Conversely, if they seem disengaged, you may need to pick up the pace or incorporate more dynamic elements into your presentation.

4. Be open to feedback: after your presentation, actively seek feedback from your audience. Ask them what they found most valuable, what could have been improved, and what additional questions they may have. This feedback can help you refine your approach for future presentations.

By developing the ability to adapt on the fly, you demonstrate your commitment to your audience's needs and your flexibility as a speaker. This responsiveness helps build trust and credibility, making your audience more likely to engage with your message and remember your key points.

Interactive Techniques

In addition to building rapport and understanding your audience, you can use various techniques to keep your listeners engaged throughout your presentation. These strategies help maintain interest, foster interaction, and ensure your message resonates with them.

Incorporating interactive elements into your presentation can transform passive listeners into active participants. By encouraging your audience to engage with your content, you create a more dynamic and memorable experience. Here are some interactive techniques to consider:

1. Live polling or surveys: use online tools or mobile apps to gather real-time feedback and opinions from your audience. This can help you gauge their understanding, preferences, or reactions to specific points during your presentation.

2. Small group discussions: divide your audience into smaller groups and assign each group a topic or question to discuss. This will encourage active participation and allow your listeners to process and apply your content in a more intimate setting.

3. Hands-on activities or demonstrations: if applicable to your topic, consider incorporating hands-on activities or demonstrations that allow your audience to experience your content firsthand. This can help reinforce your message and create a more memorable learning experience. When planning interactive elements, consider the size and composition of your audience, the time available, and the venue's logistics. Ensure the activities

are relevant to your content and contribute to your objectives. Provide clear instructions and be prepared to facilitate the interactions effectively.

4. Q&A sessions: allocate time for your audience to ask questions and share their thoughts. This not only promotes engagement but also helps you identify areas where you may need to provide clarification or additional information.

Don't shy away from Q&A sessions. Many speakers worry that they might not know all the answers to every question. That's ok. You are human; you're not an encyclopedia (although you should be familiar with your topic). Most people will appreciate your honesty. You can also turn the tables and pose thought-provoking questions throughout your presentation. Doing this lets you take the spotlight off yourself and invite your listeners to participate in learning and exploring your topic more deeply.

Here are a few good strategies for using questions effectively:

1. Open-ended questions: ask questions that require more than a simple "yes" or "no" answer. Open-ended questions encourage your audience to think more critically and share their insights and experiences.
Example: "What do you think is the biggest challenge facing our industry today and how can we address it?"

2. Rhetorical questions: use rhetorical questions to emphasize critical points or challenge your audience's assumptions. These questions can help create a sense of intrigue and encourage your listeners to consider your topic from new perspectives.
Example: "Can we really afford to ignore the implications of artificial intelligence on job markets?"

3. Follow-up questions: after an audience member asks a question, consider asking a follow-up question to clarify their point or

encourage them to elaborate. This shows that you are interested in their input and can lead to more discussion.
Example: "Thanks for your input. How do you think businesses should adapt their training programs to better prepare employees for integrating AI in the workplace?"

When asking questions, allow adequate time for your audience to respond. Embrace the silence that may follow a question, as it gives your listeners a chance to process and formulate their thoughts. If participation is low, consider rephrasing the question or providing an example to stimulate discussion.

Handling Tough Questions

No matter how well-prepared you are, there may be times when you face tough questions from your audience. These questions may challenge your ideas, point out potential weaknesses in your argument, or catch you off guard. How you handle these situations can significantly impact your credibility and the overall success of your presentation.

One of the best ways to handle tough questions is to anticipate them in advance. Before your presentation, take some time to brainstorm potential questions or concerns your audience may have. Consider the following strategies:

1. Put yourself in your audience's shoes: what questions or objections might they have based on their background, experience, or perspective?

2. Review previous feedback: re-read feedback from previous presentations on similar topics. This can give you insight into common concerns or areas of confusion.

3. Conduct thorough research on your topic: be aware of controversies or differing opinions around the topic you are

presenting. This will help you identify potential challenges and prepare thoughtful responses.

4. Ask others: share your presentation with colleagues or friends and ask them to pose challenging questions. This can help refine your responses and build your confidence.

Consider the tone or attitude behind each challenging question. Some may be asked out of genuine curiosity or a natural desire for more information, while others may be aggressive or skeptical. Preparing for a range of question types can help you feel more equipped to handle whatever comes your way.

Maintaining Composure

When faced with a tricky question, it's essential to maintain your composure and project confidence. Remember, your audience is looking to you as the expert, and how you respond can significantly influence their perception of your credibility and authority.

Here are some tips for maintaining composure and confidence:

1. Take a deep breath: pause before responding. This allows you to collect your thoughts and avoid rushing into a defensive or unclear answer.

2. Maintain eye contact: look directly at the person asking the question and turn up the corners of your mouth into a friendly smile. This demonstrates your engagement and willingness to address their concerns directly.

3. Use a calm and even tone of voice: avoid getting defensive or aggressive, even if the question seems hostile or unfair.

4. Acknowledge the validity of the question or concern. This shows that you respect your audience's input and are open to discussing different perspectives.

If you feel flustered or emotional, take a moment to regain your composure. You might say, "That's a great question, and I want to ensure I give it the thoughtful response it deserves. I will take a moment to gather my thoughts." Or "Please come and get me at the end of this session, and we can discuss this in more detail." This can buy you time to collect yourself and formulate a clear and confident response, especially if the reply is not relevant to everyone in the room.

Structuring Your Response

When answering a tricky question, I like to provide a clear and concise response directly addressing the issue. This is the structure I follow:

1. Restate the question or concern: this ensures you understood it correctly and allows you to organize your thoughts.

2. If possible, provide a direct answer to the question: if the question is more complex or open-ended, acknowledge that and offer your perspective or insights.

3. Support your answer with evidence, examples, or reasoning: this helps reinforce your credibility and shows that your response is well-thought-out and substantiated.

4. Conclude by reiterating your main point: offer to discuss the issue further after the presentation, if needed.

If you don't have a complete answer to a question, it's okay to acknowledge that. You might say, "That's a complex issue that deserves more time than we currently have. While I don't have a comprehensive answer now, I'd be happy to discuss it further after the presentation or point you towards additional resources on the topic." This shows honesty and humility while still demonstrating your willingness to engage with the question.

Turning Challenges into Opportunities

While tough questions can be intimidating, they also present opportunities to demonstrate your expertise, engage with your audience, and enhance the overall impact of your presentation. Consider the following strategies for turning challenges into opportunities:

1. Use questions as a chance to clarify or expand upon your ideas. If a question reveals a potential area of confusion, provide additional examples or explanations to help your audience better understand your message.

2. Embrace different perspectives and use them to enrich the discussion. If a question challenges your ideas, acknowledge the validity of the alternative viewpoint and explain how it relates to your position. This demonstrates your openness to diverse opinions and can lead to a more nuanced and comprehensive understanding of the topic.

3. Use questions as a springboard for further engagement. If a question sparks a lively discussion or debate, consider allocating more time for audience interaction or inviting participants to continue the conversation after the presentation.

4. Learn from the questions and feedback you receive. Use them to refine your ideas, improve your presentation skills, and better understand your audience's needs and concerns.

Remember, tough questions are not personal attacks or indictments of your expertise. They are opportunities to engage more deeply with your audience, strengthen your arguments, and leave a lasting impact. By approaching these challenges with grace, confidence, and a growth mindset, you can turn even the most difficult questions into powerful moments of connection and learning.

Dealing with Interruptions

In addition to tough questions, you may encounter interruptions or challenging behaviors from audience members during your presentation. These disruptions can take many forms, from audience members arriving late, engaging in side conversations, or phone use to more overt challenges or heckling. The first step in dealing with interruptions is identifying them early and promptly addressing them calmly and professionally.

Depending on the nature and severity of the interruption, you may choose to:

1. Pause briefly and make eye contact with the person or group causing the interruption. Often, a simple, silent acknowledgment is enough to discourage the behavior.

2. Gently remind the audience of the importance of their attention and participation. For example, you might say, "I know this is a complex topic, so I appreciate your full attention as we work through these ideas together."

3. If the interruption persists, address it more directly. You could say, "I'm sorry, but the side conversations make it difficult for others to hear. Could I please ask for your cooperation in keeping the room focused?"

If the interruption is more severe or hostile, maintain your composure and respond respectfully. Acknowledge the person's concerns, but firmly redirect the conversation to your presentation. For example, "I appreciate your perspective, but for the sake of time and staying on topic, let's discuss that further after the presentation."

Public Speaking Q&A Confidence Assessment

I have prepared a questionnaire to help you identify your strengths and areas for improvement in your approach to question-and-answer sessions.

Answer each question honestly. Choose the option that best describes your current experience and feelings.

1. **How often do you incorporate Q&A sessions into your presentations?**
   -Never
   -Rarely
   -Sometimes
   -Often
   -Always

2. **How do you feel when you think about handling a Q&A session?**
   -Very anxious
   -Somewhat anxious
   -Neutral
   -Somewhat confident
   -Very confident

3. **What aspect of Q&A sessions worry you the most?**
   -Not knowing the answer
   -Handling hostile questions
   -Keeping the session on track
   -Managing time effectively
   -Engaging a quiet audience

4. **How prepared do you feel to handle unexpected questions?**
   -Not prepared at all
   -Slightly prepared
   -Moderately prepared
   -Very prepared
   -Extremely prepared

5. **Have you ever been unable to answer a question during a session? If yes, how did you handle it?**
   -Yes, I admitted I didn't know the answer.
   -Yes, I deferred the answer to a later time.
   -Yes, I redirected the question to the audience.
   -No, I've always had an answer.

6. **How much do you prepare for potential questions before your presentations?**
   -I don't prepare at all.
   -I think about a few possible questions.
   -I extensively prepare for many possible questions.
   -I prepare with mock Q&A sessions.

7. **Do you use any specific techniques to engage the audience during Q&A sessions?**
   -No, I don't use any specific techniques.
   -Yes, I use direct questions to prompt participation.
   -Yes, I use interactive tools like live polls.
   -Yes, I encourage audience members to discuss among themselves first.

8. **How do you usually manage hostile or aggressive questions?**
   -I get flustered and struggle to respond.
   -I move on to another question quickly.
   -I address the question calmly and professionally.
   -I invite the questioner to discuss it privately after the session.

9. **What feedback have you received from audiences about your Q&A sessions?**
   -Mostly negative.
   -Somewhat negative.
   -Mixed reviews.
   -Mostly positive.
   -I haven't received any feedback.

10. **What would help you feel more confident during Q&A sessions?**
    -More subject matter expertise.
    -Techniques for managing stress and anxiety.
    -Better strategies for engaging the audience.
    -Training on handling difficult questions.
    -More experience with actual Q&A sessions.

Your answers will paint a clear picture of your current attitude to Q&A sessions and highlight what needs improvement so you can work on that area for future presentations.

Building Long-term Relationships

Effectively handling challenging situations is not just about managing the moment; it's also about building long-term relationships with your audience. You can establish yourself as a trusted and respected speaker by demonstrating your professionalism, expertise, and commitment to their learning and growth.

Here are some strategies for building long-term relationships with your audience:

1. Follow up after the presentation. Send a thank-you email to participants, share additional resources or materials related to your topic, and invite them to connect with you on professional networks like LinkedIn.

2. Seek feedback and use it to improve. Ask your audience for honest feedback on your presentation and use their input to refine your content and delivery for future engagements.

3. Stay engaged and accessible. Remember, it's all about building rapport with the people in the room. The more your audience knows you, the more they will like you. The more they like you,

the more they will trust you. When they trust you, they will listen to you, buy from you, follow you, and write great reviews about you!

Public speaking is a profoundly rewarding experience but also filled with challenges. Embracing the unexpected elements and interacting meaningfully with your audience can significantly enrich your presentation and your growth as a speaker. As mentioned, building rapport creates a foundational connection that enhances receptivity to your message, while thorough audience analysis ensures your content resonates deeper.

By mastering the strategies discussed in this chapter, you will be better equipped to navigate any speaking environment, ensuring that each presentation is effective and a genuine exchange of ideas and perspectives takes place. Remember, every challenge is a chance to shine, and every interaction is a step toward becoming a more impactful and inspiring speaker.

Embrace these opportunities with a positive outlook, and your public speaking journey will be an exciting adventure of continuous learning and connection.

9

EFFECTIVE USE OF TECHNOLOGY AND VISUAL AIDS

"The more striking your presentation, the more people will remember you." P Arden

In his 2006 TED Talk, Swedish physician and statistician Hans Rosling used data visualization to challenge common misconceptions about global health and development. Throughout his presentation, "The Best Stats You've Ever Seen," Rosling used Gapminder, a software tool he co-developed, to display animated bubble charts that illustrate complex data clearly and engagingly. Rosling guided the audience through a compelling narrative by interacting with the visualizations in real time, revealing surprising trends and insights. The dynamic nature of the presentation kept the audience engaged and helped them grasp the key messages quickly.

I share this with you because Rosling's talk, although old, showcases the power visual aids can have to elevate a presentation from merely informative to genuinely influential. When employed strategically, visual aids can capture the audience's attention, reinforce an important message, and forge a deep connection between the listeners and the shared ideas. Each slide or prop you use should be thoughtfully selected to work harmoniously with your spoken words, complementing and amplifying their impact, not distracting or interrupting your flow.

This chapter will examine everything from basic visual aids like photographs to more advanced technologies. You will learn how to choose the right visual aids for your next presentation, understand design principles, and respond when things go wrong with technology.

Optimal Visual Aid

A diverse array of visual aids exist and are at your disposal as a speaker, ranging from simple graphs to intricate animations. The key to success is identifying the type that most effectively conveys your intended message. As mentioned above, a well-designed graph can distill the information into an easily digestible format when faced with complex data. Alternatively, a flowchart or timeline may prove more suitable when explaining a process or sequence of events.

Photographs can inject a personal touch or evoke an emotional response, while diagrams illustrate a whole's components. With their dynamic nature, videos introduce movement and can immediately captivate an audience's attention. The selection of appropriate visual aids requires an understanding of the subject matter and the audience's needs and preferences.

Before settling on a specific visual, it is crucial to consider the takeaway you want the audience to gain from each one. Is the goal to provide clarity, create impact, or leave a lasting impression? This deliberation ensures that the chosen visuals are not mere embellishments but integral elements that enhance and support the narrative.

Design Principles

The impact of a visual aid depends on its design. Fundamental design principles such as balance, contrast, alignment, and repetition significantly influence how the audience perceives and engages with the visuals. A well-balanced design ensures that no single element overpowers the others, allowing the information to be easily absorbed.

Contrast can highlight key points, such as critical data in a chart. Consistent alignment creates a clean and organized appearance, making complex information more accessible to digest. Repetition of style or color across visuals enhances the overall cohesiveness of the presentation, reinforcing the central message (and your brand) through visual consistency.

When designing visuals, it is crucial to prioritize legibility and simplicity. Cluttered visuals with excessive text or data can lead to confusion. Opting for easily readable fonts and appropriate sizes ensures the information is visible even from a distance. Simplicity in design often translates to clear communication, ensuring that the visuals both engage and inform the audience. If design is not your natural talent, I recommend hiring a professional. Once you have a great template, you can use it repeatedly.

An example of effective visual design that comes to mind is Apple, known for its sleek, minimalist presentations. Their iPhone launch event slides are often nothing more than a striking product image against a plain background with a single, powerful phrase. By stripping away irrelevant elements, Apple ensures the audience focuses solely on the product and its key features. The visuals complement the message rather than competing with it.

Ensuring Everybody Can Engage

Inclusivity is vital in presentations. You want everyone in your audience to be able to engage with your visuals, including those with disabilities. By incorporating the following, you respect your entire audience and ensure your message reaches everyone effectively.

1. Provide alternative text for images so screen readers can describe them.

2. Use color schemes that are friendly to colorblind individuals.

3. Caption your videos for those with hearing impairments.

4. Ensure audience seating allows everyone a clear view of the visuals.

Videos and other multimedia can be game changers in presentations, but only when used effectively. Here are some dos and don'ts to keep in mind:

- Do choose multimedia that directly supports your objectives.

- Do ensure the content is high-quality and professionally produced.

- Do consider your audience's cultural and demographic background when selecting multimedia.

- Do introduce each multimedia element with context to integrate it seamlessly into your narrative.

- Do use multimedia to re-engage the audience during lengthy or data-heavy sections.

- Do test your multimedia beforehand. Technical glitches can derail even the best presentations.

- Don't use multimedia just for the sake of it. Each element should serve a clear purpose.

- Don't let multimedia overshadow your main message. It should enhance, not distract.

- Don't rely on multimedia alone. Your presentation should stand on its own, even without the fancy extras.

Here are some tools I've used in the past.

Software:

1. PowerPoint and Keynote: for creating slides and integrating multimedia.

2. Prezi: a cloud-based presentation tool that allows dynamic, non-linear presentations.

3. Canva: a graphic design tool for creating visually appealing slides and infographics.

4. Adobe Creative Suite: for video editing, graphic design, and animation.

Online Platforms:

1. SlideShare: for sharing and discovering presentations, infographics, and documents.

2. Vimeo and YouTube: allow for easy embedding of videos into presentations.

3. Mentimeter and Slido: enable live polls, Q&A sessions, and audience engagement.

4. Piktochart and Infogram: these create interactive infographics and data visualizations.

Re-engagement Through Multimedia

Multimedia can be particularly effective in re-engaging an audience that might be losing focus. A relevant video or an interactive element can revitalize the audience's attention and interest following a deep dive into detailed data or a prolonged speech section. This strategy works by providing a change in stimulus. Interactive elements, such as audience response systems that complement the multimedia, draw attention and actively involve the audience in the presentation, making the experience more participatory.

Multimedia offers a powerful storytelling tool that can evoke emotions and create a strong connection with the audience. Whether it's a customer testimonial, a dramatic re-enactment, or an animated story, these formats can compellingly convey your message, making the underlying concepts more relatable and accessible.

Technical Considerations

No matter how great your visuals are, technical issues can negatively affect your confidence and destroy your presentation. To ensure a smooth delivery, remember the following:

1. Always have a backup: save your presentation on multiple devices and bring printouts of slides, just in case.

2. Test, test, test: check your visuals on the equipment you'll be using, including the projector and sound system. Iron out any glitches before showtime.

3. Arrive early: give yourself ample time to set up and troubleshoot issues before your audience arrives.

4. Know your tools: familiarize yourself with the presentation software and equipment you'll be using. Practice navigating your slides and adjusting settings.

5. Have a plan B: if technical difficulties arise mid-presentation, don't panic. Have a joke or anecdote ready to keep the audience engaged while you resolve the issue.

Even with the best preparations, sometimes things go wrong. I once attended a conference where the keynote speaker's microphone died mid-sentence. Instead of panicking, she stepped forward, looked around, projected her voice, and said, "Well, I guess this is the universe's way of telling me to speak up!" The audience smiled, and she continued without missing a beat. Her quick wit and adaptability turned a potentially disastrous moment into a memorable one. Technical issues will happen. It's how you handle them that matters. You can gracefully navigate any presentation pitfall by staying calm, keeping your sense of humor, and having a backup plan.

Leveraging Social Media

Social media is a powerful tool for enhancing the reach and impact of public speaking engagements. By leveraging social media platforms, you can extend the life cycle of your presentations, from building anticipation before the event to continuing the conversation long after its conclusion. This amplifies your message and strengthens your connection with the audience.

The phase before the presentation offers a valuable opportunity to set the stage and cultivate the audience's interest and excitement. Share snippets of your upcoming talk to spark curiosity and build anticipation. Consider sharing short teaser videos, intriguing quotes, or critical questions the presentation addresses. These serve as appetizers, providing enough information to whet the audience's appetite for the main course. Another great strategy is creating event pages or groups where attendees can RSVP, share the event, and engage in preliminary discussions. This boosts the event's visibility and initiates audience engagement before the presentation.

Integrating live social media interaction into your presentation can significantly enhance audience engagement and participation. Encouraging live sharing of the presentation using a specific hashtag allows online followers to participate in real-time, even if they are not physically present, and enables a broader discussion that can extend the reach of the talk. Displaying live social media posts on a screen beside the presentation fosters more interaction, as participants see their contributions acknowledged in real-time.

After the presentation, social media is an excellent platform to continue dialogue and deepen your relationship with the audience. Start by sharing a thank-you post on various platforms and acknowledging the audience's participation and feedback. Following this, share key highlights or segments of the presentation that were particularly well-received. This serves as a refresher for attendees and provides value to those unable to attend.

To foster ongoing engagement, consider releasing additional content related to the presentation topic over the following weeks. This could be in the form of blog posts, infographics, or follow-up videos. This content keeps the conversation alive, reinforcing the key messages of the talk and providing additional value to the audience. Ensure you actively engage by responding to these posts' comments, questions, and discussions. This will demonstrate a genuine commitment to the audience beyond the presentation itself.

Use this worksheet to plan and execute a social media strategy to increase engagement for your next presentation:

1. Identify key questions or ideas from the presentation to share on social media to generate interest.

2. Create visually appealing content (images, videos, infographics) to promote the upcoming talk.

3. Select appropriate platforms and create event pages or groups.

4. Develop relevant questions for social media polls to gather audience insights.

5. Choose a unique and memorable hashtag for the presentation.

6. Plan to integrate the live social media feed into the presentation.

7. Select suitable tools for conducting live surveys or Q&A sessions.

8. Develop strategies to encourage participation throughout.

9. Identify the main takeaways from the presentation to share on social media afterward.

10. Create additional content (blog posts, videos, infographics) to add value.

11. Develop a promotion strategy to share post-presentation content with the audience.

12. Respond to comments and questions on the shared content.

By strategically leveraging social media platforms, you can amplify the impact of your presentation, foster meaningful connections with your audience, and extend the reach of your message beyond the event itself. I encourage you to embrace social media and use it to engage, inspire, and build a community around your ideas and expertise.

The Future of Public Speaking

Integrating advanced technologies such as Virtual Reality (VR) and Artificial Intelligence (AI) is revolutionizing how we prepare, deliver and personalize presentations. These technologies offer new frontiers in enhancing speaker training, optimizing engagement, and tailoring content to meet each audience member's unique preferences and needs. As we navigate this exciting era, understanding the application and implications of these technologies is paramount for anyone seeking to excel in public speaking.

Virtual Reality provides an immersive environment to hone your public speaking skills. By simulating diverse speaking environments, from a small boardroom to a packed conference hall, VR allows you to practice your delivery in a controlled yet realistic setting. This technology will enable you to rehearse your speech and interact with varied audience types and sizes. VR can also provide real-time feedback on your body language, eye contact, and engagement as you address a virtual audience that reacts like a live crowd. This feedback is invaluable, as it allows for adjustments in performance that traditional practice settings might not. For instance, VR can simulate a distracted audience, allowing you to master techniques to recapture attention. Repeating scenarios within these virtual environments can significantly enhance your speaking confidence and competence.

AI-driven Analytics

Artificial Intelligence transforms public speaking by providing precise and tailored analytics. AI tools can analyze various presentation aspects, from speech patterns and pacing to audience engagement levels. For example, AI can identify parts of the speech where engagement drops, allowing you to refine these areas for a more significant impact. It can also provide feedback on pacing, suggesting adjustments to ensure that the delivery matches the intended emotional tone of each segment. In addition, AI-driven analysis can evaluate the audience's reactions, providing a deeper understanding of how the message is received and what emotions it evokes. This real-time data is so helpful in allowing you to adjust your delivery and enhance the overall effectiveness of your communication.

Personalization and AI

AI excels in its ability to personalize content, ensuring that each audience member receives a message that resonates with them. By analyzing data points from previous interactions, AI can help tailor your presentation to better align with your audience's interests, knowledge level, and cultural background. For example, AI can modify your slide show in real time to include more basic explanations if the audience needs to become more familiar with the terminology. Alternatively, you could adjust the cultural references in your speech to better match the predominant demographics of your audience. This level of customization not only improves audience comprehension but also significantly boosts engagement.

Ethical Considerations

While the benefits of VR and AI in public speaking are substantial, they also present ethical considerations that must be carefully considered. One primary concern is privacy; as AI technologies often collect and analyze large amounts of data, it is essential to ensure that this data is handled in alignment with privacy laws and ethical standards. Transparency with your audience about what data is being collected and how it is used is essential to maintain trust.

Additionally, there is the risk of overreliance on technology, which could diminish your genuine interaction with the audience. While these tools are potent, they should enhance rather than replace the human elements of public speaking.

As you refine your skills in this area, consider each presentation an opportunity to experiment with new tools and techniques to enhance your effectiveness as a speaker. I encourage you to be open to evolving with the changing landscape of technology in this area.

Crafting Engaging Slideshows – A Speakers Guide

Slideshows are a staple in the world of presentations, but let's face it – we've all experienced "death by PowerPoint." So here is a summary of creating slideshows that engage and educate.

1. Less really is more: limit text on each slide. Use large, plain font. Use concise bullet points, not paragraphs.

2. Visuals over text: whenever possible, convey information using images, graphs, or charts. Visuals are processed faster and remembered longer than text.

3. Consistency is vital: maintain a consistent theme, font, and color scheme throughout your slides. This creates a professional, cohesive look.

4. Embed multimedia wisely: videos and animations can add interest and break up text-heavy sections. But use them sparingly and ensure they're relevant to your message.

5. Tell a story: structure your slides to follow a logical narrative arc. Each slide should build upon the previous one, leading your audience towards your key takeaways.

6. Practice, practice, practice: familiarize yourself with your slides and the flow of your presentation. This will allow you to focus on engaging with your audience rather than fumbling with technology.

As you move forward in your public speaking journey, remember that visual aids are tools to support your message, not to replace it. Your words, passion, and connection with the audience remain the heart of any excellent presentation. Use these visual techniques to amplify your message, but keep them from overshadowing your unique voice and perspective.

In the end, the most effective presentations strike a balance between compelling content, engaging delivery, and supportive visuals. By mastering the art of visual aids, you're equipping yourself with a powerful tool to captivate your audience and leave a lasting impression.

Your presentations will naturally become more engaging as you refine your skills, embrace new technologies, and experiment with different visual techniques.

10

Tailoring Your Message Across Various Contexts

"If you can't say it, you can't sell it!" A Robinson

As a public speaker, your ability to adapt your message, delivery style, and engagement techniques to suit different purposes can significantly impact your success in achieving your communication goals. This chapter will delve into the unique considerations and strategies for delivering impactful speeches and presentations in various settings, including business pitches, workshops and seminars, social events, and inspirational talks. By understanding the nuances of each context and employing tailored techniques, you can build stronger connections with your audience, convey your message more effectively, and leave a lasting impact on your listeners.

Structuring A Business Pitch

Crafting a successful business pitch goes beyond assembling facts and figures; it involves structuring your content to resonate with your audience and achieve your strategic goals. Begin by defining the purpose of your presentation clearly—is it to inform, persuade, or propose? Once the purpose is clear, tailor your content to align with your audience's interests, emphasizing how your message addresses their needs or solves their problems.

A well-structured business pitch typically starts with an introduction that captures attention and outlines the discussion topics. This is followed by the body of the presentation, where key arguments are presented logically and supported by data and insights. Each main point should seamlessly connect to the next, maintaining a narrative flow that guides the audience through your reasoning. The conclusion briefly summarizes the main points and ends with a solid call to action. It prompts the audience to take a specific step, be it approval, a follow-up meeting, or direct action related to the business proposal.

Frame your business solutions within a story that illustrates the challenges faced, the actions taken, and the results achieved. This will make your presentation more engaging and help the audience visualize your proposals' practical application and impact.

A notable example of a successful business pitch is Airbnb's pitch to investors in 2009. Brian Chesky, the co-founder of Airbnb, crafted a compelling narrative highlighting the problem the company aimed to solve: the lack of affordable and unique accommodation options for travelers. He began by sharing his personal story of struggling to pay rent and coming up with the idea of renting out air mattresses in his apartment to conference attendees.

Throughout the pitch, Chesky uses emotional appeals to connect with investors, describing the frustrations and desires of modern travelers seeking authentic experiences. He supported these emotional appeals with logical evidence, presenting market research and data demonstrating the growing demand for alternative accommodations. Chesky also addressed potential concerns by discussing the company's safety measures and insurance policies, building credibility and trust with the investors.

To further engage the audience, Chesky used visuals, including photos of Airbnb listings and customer testimonials, to illustrate the platform's unique value proposition. He concluded the pitch with a solid call to action, inviting investors to join Airbnb in revolutionizing the travel industry and creating unforgettable experiences for millions worldwide. As a result of this effective pitch, Airbnb secured $600,000 in funding, setting the stage for its future success as a global hospitality platform.

Delivering Engaging Workshops and Seminars

Professional development workshops and seminars are pivotal platforms for interactive learning and knowledge sharing. The success of these events hinges significantly on your ability to deliver content that holds participants' attention, encourages their active involvement, and facilitates real-time learning. This requires a deliberate approach where every element of the workshop or seminar is designed to foster engagement and comprehension.

Interactive elements are the cornerstone of engaging workshops and seminars. They transform passive listening into active learning and foster a collaborative environment that encourages participation. Techniques such as breakout sessions allow participants to delve into specific topics in smaller groups, facilitating deeper discussion and problem-solving. These sessions can be efficient when participants are asked to tackle a relevant challenge or develop a strategy based on the session's content, applying what they've learned in a practical context.

Incorporating gamification elements such as quizzes or competitive team activities can energize participants and make learning fun and impactful. These activities should be closely aligned with the learning objectives of the seminar or workshop, ensuring that they reinforce the core content while also adding an element of enjoyment.

Educational Content Delivery

Educational content delivered in workshops and seminars must be explicit, engaging, and paced appropriately to suit your audience's learning styles and preferences. Start by clearly outlining the session's objectives, what participants can expect to learn, and how to apply this knowledge professionally. This sets the stage for meaningful engagement as participants understand the value of the presented information.

Using a variety of presentation methods can help cater to different learning styles. For example, visual learners benefit from charts, diagrams, and videos, while auditory learners may gain more from discussions and lectures. Kinesthetic learners, who learn best through doing, will appreciate interactive activities that involve physical participation or hands-on experiments. It's also good to intersperse theoretical information with real-life case studies or anecdotes, which can help ground abstract concepts in practical reality. These stories should be relevant and relatable, ideally reflecting professional scenarios that participants might encounter.

Inviting questions and facilitating discussions throughout the session is crucial rather than saving all questions for the end. This keeps the content dynamic and responsive to the participants' needs, allowing for immediate clarification and deeper exploration of complex topics. Encourage participants to share their experiences or perspectives on the content, fostering a peer-learning environment where participants can learn from each other and you.

Participant Engagement

Maximizing participant engagement in workshops and seminars involves creating an environment where participants feel comfortable, curious, and motivated to engage. Begin by establishing a welcoming atmosphere where all participants feel valued and encouraged to contribute. This can be achieved by actively listening to their contributions, acknowledging different viewpoints, and integrating diverse participant experiences into the session's content.

Effective facilitation techniques also play a crucial role in maintaining engagement. This includes managing the room's energy levels by incorporating physical movement or changes in activity type when energy wanes. Techniques such as think-pair-share, where participants first think about a question individually, then discuss their thoughts with a partner, and finally share with the larger group, can stimulate engagement and ensure that more introverted participants also have a voice.

Feedback and Evaluation

Gathering and implementing feedback is essential for continuously improving your workshops and seminars. Provide participants multiple opportunities to give input throughout the session to gauge immediate reactions.

To gather constructive feedback after a workshop or seminar, consider asking the following questions:

1. What were the most valuable insights or takeaways from the session?

2. How relevant and applicable was the content to your professional or personal life?

3. What aspects of the presentation style and delivery most engaged you?

4. Were there any topics or concepts that needed more clarification or depth?

5. How effectively did the interactive elements (e.g., group discussions and exercises) contribute to your learning experience?

6. On a scale of 1-5, how would you rate the overall quality and value of the workshop/seminar?

7. What suggestions do you have for improving the content or delivery of future sessions?

When analyzing the feedback, start by organizing the responses into categories or themes, such as content relevance, presentation style, interactivity, and areas for improvement. Look for patterns or recurring comments that indicate strengths or weaknesses in specific aspects of the workshop or seminar. For quantitative questions, such as rating the overall quality, calculate the average score to gauge general satisfaction levels. Pay close attention to extreme ratings (very high or low) and the accompanying comments to identify notable successes or areas that require significant improvement. Prioritize the feedback based on the frequency and urgency of the comments. For example, if many participants mentioned that a particular topic needed more depth, consider expanding on that subject in future sessions. Similarly, if several people praised a specific interactive exercise, look for ways to incorporate similar activities in other workshops or seminars.

When acting upon the feedback, communicate the planned changes or improvements to the participants, demonstrating their input is valued and taken seriously. This transparency and responsiveness will foster a sense of engagement and investment in the learning process, encouraging participants to provide feedback in the future.

Toasts & Tributes: Speaking from the Heart

Before you start writing a social speech, it's crucial to understand your audience and the occasion. Ask yourself: Who will be attending the event? What is the purpose of the gathering? Is it a wedding, a retirement party, or a milestone celebration? By clearly understanding your audience and the event's significance, you can tailor your message to strike the right tone and connect with your listeners on a deeper level.

When it comes to social speeches, authenticity is critical. Your words should come from the heart, reflecting your genuine feelings and emotions. To ensure your message is heartfelt, take some time to reflect on your relationship with the person or group you're honoring. Think about the moments you've shared, the qualities you admire, and their impact on your life. By tapping into these personal experiences, you'll be able to craft a message that is both sincere and meaningful.

Aim for a balanced structure that combines emotion, humor, and sincerity to create a toast or tribute that captivates your audience. Here's a suggested outline:

1. Opening: begin with a warm greeting and express your gratitude for the opportunity to speak.

2. Personal Connection: share a brief story or anecdote highlighting your relationship with the honored person or group.

3. Admirable Qualities: highlight the qualities or achievements that make the honoree unique. Use specific examples to illustrate your points.

4. Humor: inject humor to keep the mood light and to engage. Choose appropriate and respectful anecdotes or jokes.

5. Heartfelt Wishes: express your hopes and wishes for the honoree's future. Offer words of encouragement and support.

6. Toast or Tribute: conclude by inviting everyone to raise their glasses or join you in paying tribute to the honoree.

Personal stories and anecdotes can make your toast or tribute more engaging and relatable. When selecting stories to share, consider moments that showcase the honoree's character, achievements, or impact on others. Aim for concise, relevant, and emotionally resonant stories. To seamlessly incorporate personal stories into your speech, use transitional phrases like "I remember when..." or "One moment that stands out to me is..." These phrases help to weave the stories into the overall narrative of your tribute, making it feel cohesive and natural.

Delivering a toast or tribute with confidence requires practice. Start by writing out your speech and reading it aloud several times. Pay attention to your pacing, intonation, and emphasis on critical points. As you become more comfortable with the content, practice delivering the speech without relying on your notes. Consider recording yourself or practicing in front of a mirror to observe your body language and facial expressions. Aim for a natural and conversational delivery, making eye contact with your audience and speaking from the heart. Remember, the goal is not perfection but authenticity. Your audience will appreciate your effort in crafting a heartfelt message, even if there are a few stumbles.

Eulogies: Honoring Memories with Words

When tasked with writing a eulogy, gather memories, anecdotes, and insights from those who knew the deceased best. Reach out to family members, close friends, and colleagues to collect stories and reflections that capture the essence of the person's life.

Begin by asking open-ended questions like, "What are some of your fondest memories with [name]?" or "How did [name] impact your life?" Encourage people to share specific stories, quirky habits, or memorable moments that showcase the deceased's personality, values, and achievements. As you gather these stories, look for common themes that can help you paint a complete picture of the person's life. These insights will be the foundation for a eulogy that truly honors their memory.

A eulogy is a delicate balance between expressing grief and celebrating the life and achievements of the deceased. While it's important to acknowledge the sorrow and loss felt by those left behind, it's equally crucial to focus on the person's positive impact during their lifetime. Begin by acknowledging the sadness and pain of the moment, but gradually shift the focus to the joy, laughter, and love that the person brought into the world. Share stories highlighting their kindness, generosity, and unique qualities that made them special. Emphasize how the deceased made a difference in the lives of others, whether through their career, hobbies, or personal relationships.

By celebrating their accomplishments and the love they shared, you create a tone that is both respectful and uplifting, reminding everyone of the beautiful life that was lived.

Structuring the Eulogy

When crafting a eulogy, aim for a flow that seamlessly weaves memories, personal reflections, and tributes together. Here's a suggested outline:

1. Introduction: begin by expressing gratitude for the opportunity to speak and your relationship with the deceased.

2. Early Life and Childhood: share stories or anecdotes from the person's early years, highlighting their upbringing and formative experiences.

3. Personal Qualities and Values: discuss the qualities and values that defined the deceased, using examples to illustrate their character.

4. Achievements and Contributions: highlight the person's personal and professional accomplishments and their impact on others.

5. Memories and Anecdotes: share specific stories and memories that capture the person's essence, evoking laughter and tears.

6. Legacy and Lasting Impact: reflect on how the deceased's life will continue to inspire and influence those they left behind.

7. Closing: offer comfort and support to the grieving audience, acknowledging the collective loss while celebrating the gift of the person's life.

Delivering a eulogy is emotional and challenging, but it's also an opportunity to connect with the audience and offer comfort during a difficult time. When giving the eulogy, prioritize empathy, respect, and sincerity. Speak from the heart, allowing your emotions to show while maintaining composure. Make eye contact with the audience, engaging them with your words and presence. Pause when necessary to gather your thoughts or allow moments of reflection.

Remember, the purpose of the eulogy is to honor the deceased and provide solace to those grieving. By speaking with authenticity and compassion, you create a safe space for everyone to mourn, remember, and celebrate the life of their loved one.

Master of Ceremonies

A master of ceremonies plays a pivotal role in setting the tone, guiding the flow, and ensuring the success of an event. As an MC, your primary responsibilities include:

1. Welcoming and engaging the audience.

2. Introducing speakers, performers, or special guests.

3. Keeping the event on schedule and managing transitions.

4. Facilitating audience participation and interaction.

5. Handling any unexpected situations or changes with grace and composure.

Preparing and organizing the event segments thoroughly ensures a smooth flow and engaging experience. Start by familiarizing yourself with the event's agenda, including the order of speakers, performances, or activities.

Collaborate with the event organizers to understand each segment's purpose and goals. This knowledge will allow you to create seamless transitions and provide context for the audience.

Prepare introductions for each speaker or performer, highlighting their background, accomplishments, and relevance to the event. Practice delivering these introductions with enthusiasm and clarity. Consider adding personal anecdotes or humorous remarks to make the introductions more engaging. Ensure that any humor is appropriate and respectful to the audience and the event's tone.

Energizing the Audience

As an MC, one of your primary goals is to keep the audience engaged and energized throughout the event. Here are some techniques to achieve this:

1. Start strong: begin the event with a warm welcome and a captivating opening remark that sets the tone and captures the audience's attention.

2. Use inclusive language: address the audience as a collective, using phrases like "we" and "us" to create a sense of unity and shared experience.

3. Encourage participation: invite the audience to ask questions, share their thoughts, or participate in interactive activities when appropriate.

4. Inject humor: use appropriate and tasteful humor to keep the atmosphere light and enjoyable. However, be mindful of the event's tone and the audience's sensibilities.

5. Maintain energy: keep your energy level high throughout the event, using vocal inflections, gestures, and facial expressions to convey enthusiasm and engagement.

Building Confidence

Confidence is critical to being a successful MC. To build and maintain confidence, thoroughly prepare and practice your role. Familiarize yourself with the event's agenda, the speakers' backgrounds, and any technical aspects of the event.

Arrive at the event venue early to get comfortable with the stage, microphone, and audio-visual equipment. Practice your introductions and transitions and visualize yourself delivering them with poise and clarity. Despite thorough preparation, unexpected situations may arise during the event. An MC must think on their feet and handle these situations with composure. If a speaker runs over time, politely remind them to wrap up. If technical difficulties occur, keep the audience engaged with impromptu remarks or activities.

Remember, the audience looks to the MC for guidance and reassurance. By maintaining a calm and confident outlook, you can navigate any challenges and ensure the event continues smoothly.

Inspirational Speeches

The foundation of any inspirational speech lies in its central message—a clear, compelling idea that resonates with the audience and inspires them to take action. To identify your central message, consider the following:

1. Purpose: what is the goal of your speech? What do you want your audience to feel, think, or do differently after hearing your words?

2. Audience: who are you speaking to? What are their needs, aspirations, and challenges? How can your message address these factors?

3. Personal experience: what personal stories, insights, or lessons have shaped your perspective on the topic? How can you use these experiences to connect with your audience?

Incorporating Motivational Stories

Personal and others' motivational stories are powerful tools for illustrating key points and inspiring audiences. When selecting stories to include in your speech, look for those that:

1. Reinforce your central message.

2. Demonstrate the power of perseverance, resilience, or transformation.

3. Evoke solid emotions and create a lasting impact.

When sharing personal stories, be vulnerable and authentic. Allow your audience to see the challenges you've faced and the lessons you've learned. This vulnerability creates a bond with your listeners and makes your message more relatable. When incorporating stories of others, choose examples that are relevant and inspiring to your audience. These could be well-known figures or heroes who have overcome adversity or achieved remarkable feats. Use vivid descriptions and sensory details to bring these stories to life, allowing your audience to experience the emotions and lessons vicariously.

An inspirational speech should motivate and mobilize the audience to take concrete steps inspired by your message. As you near the end of your speech, focus on delivering a powerful call to action. Clearly articulate the specific actions you want your audience to take. These could be internal shifts in mindset or external steps towards a goal. Use robust and action-oriented language to convey a sense of urgency and possibility. Paint a vivid picture of the positive impact these actions can have on the audience's lives and the world around them. Help them envision the transformation that awaits them when they embrace your message.

Finally, leave your audience with a memorable and uplifting closing statement that encapsulates the essence of your message and inspires and empowers them.

As you can see throughout this chapter, effective communication is more than one-size-fits-all. A successful business pitch requires a blend of persuasive techniques, data-driven arguments, and a clear call to action. Workshops and seminars demand interactive elements, engaging content delivery, and continuous participant engagement. Social speeches, such as toasts and eulogies, call for heartfelt sincerity, personal anecdotes, and a delicate balance of emotions.

The key to success across all these contexts lies in understanding your audience, crafting a message that resonates with them, and delivering it authentically and confidently. Whether you're presenting in a boardroom, facilitating a workshop, delivering a toast at a wedding, or inspiring a crowd, your ability to adapt your content and style to the situation will set you apart as a versatile and impactful speaker.

As you continue to grow as a public speaker, embrace each opportunity to speak in different contexts as a chance to refine your skills further. With practice, preparation, and a willingness to adapt, you'll find that you can captivate and influence audiences in any setting, making your voice heard and your message remembered.

11

SPECIALIZED TECHNIQUES FOR DIFFERENT AUDIENCES

"Diversity is a fact, inclusion is an act." V Myers

Navigating the complexities of audience diversity is crucial in today's globalized environment. This chapter explores how to adapt your presentations to technical and non-technical audiences while also considering factors like gender, cultural backgrounds, age, disabilities, and the unique dynamics of online environments. Understanding and addressing these elements can dramatically enhance the effectiveness of your communication. There are practical tips and case studies included that illustrate how these strategies are applied in real-world scenarios.

Technical vs. Non-Technical Audiences

When you present, whether it's to a boardroom of executives or a community hall filled with locals, understanding the level of technical expertise in your audience is crucial. This understanding directly influences how you craft and deliver your message to ensure it resonates effectively. Techniques for assessing the technical level of your audience can be as straightforward as conducting pre-event surveys or as interactive as initial probing questions during the presentation itself. These strategies provide a clearer picture of whom you're addressing, allowing you to gauge the familiarity with the subject matter across your audience. For instance, in a technical presentation about cybersecurity, you might start with a question about standard cybersecurity practices to understand how deeply you should dive into the technical details.

Once you grasp the audience's expertise, simplifying complex information becomes your crucial tool in ensuring clarity and engagement, especially with non-technical listeners. Simplification involves distilling information to its essence without stripping away its meaning. This can be achieved through analogies that relate complex ideas to everyday experiences, thus making them more accessible. For example, explaining data encryption in terms of translating a secret language can help lay audiences understand its importance and function without needing to grasp its intricate mathematics. Using clear, jargon-free language is imperative. Replace technical terms with simpler words or, if specialized terms are necessary, define them succinctly at their first use.

Engagement strategies must also be tailored to fit the technical understanding of your audience. For technical audiences, deep dives into the specifics of a topic can stimulate discussion and foster engagement. These audiences appreciate the challenge of complex problems and often value data-driven insights that can lead to innovative solutions. For non-technical audiences, engagement is usually boosted through storytelling that highlights the human impact of the technology or process being discussed. Here, the focus shifts from the 'how' to the 'why' and 'what'—why the topic matters and its implications on a personal or societal level. Creating interactive segments where the audience can ask questions or share experiences can also maintain engagement, providing a platform to connect the dots in a familiar context.

Choosing the right visual aids and examples is pivotal in bridging the comprehension gap for different audience types. Visual aids for a technical audience might include detailed graphs, flowcharts, and schematics that provide in-depth analysis of data or processes. These visuals should be precise and thorough, offering the depth of information that a technically adept audience would appreciate. Conversely, visuals should emphasize clarity and impact over complexity for non-technical audiences. Infographics, highlighting key points, simple charts tracking trends, and images illustrating outcomes or benefits help make abstract concepts tangible. When selecting examples, ensure they are relatable to the audience's experiences. For instance, when explaining a technical product to non-technical users, choose examples that show practical applications of the technology in their daily lives or familiar settings, demystifying complex functionalities and highlighting real-world utility.

Gender-Specific Strategies

Understanding and respecting gender-specific communication styles is essential to crafting presentations that resonate with diverse audiences. Gender can influence how people perceive information, their preferred communication styles, and their interactions during presentations. To communicate effectively across genders, it's vital to recognize these differences and adapt your approach to be inclusive and effective.

Research has shown that communication styles can vary significantly across genders. Men often employ a more assertive and competitive communication style, which is direct and to the point. They tend to focus on independence and achieving tangible outcomes. Women, on the other hand, generally utilize a more collaborative and inclusive style. This approach emphasizes emotional connection, process orientation, and mutual understanding, often focusing on building relationships and fostering group harmony. Of course, these tendencies are not absolute and can vary widely among individuals. However, recognizing the possibility of this spectrum within gender communication styles is important; it involves observing how your audience interacts, listening to the questions they ask, and noting the feedback they provide. This understanding allows you to tailor your presentation to match or complement the predominant communication styles of your audience, ensuring that your message is heard and appreciated across gender lines.

Inclusive language plays a pivotal role in engaging all audience members effectively. It involves using terms and references that do not assume or favor one gender over another. For instance, using 'spokesperson' instead of 'spokesman' or 'chairperson' instead of 'chairman' avoids gender bias and promotes equality. The importance of inclusive language extends beyond mere political correctness. It reflects respect for the diversity within your audience and contributes to a more positive reception of your message. Inclusive language fosters an environment where all participants feel valued and respected, which can enhance their engagement and openness to you and the information presented.

Adapting your presentation style to communicate across genders effectively involves more than adjusting your language; it also includes modifying your delivery and interaction techniques. For example, when presenting to an audience that appreciates direct communication (often associated with masculine communication styles), it might be practical to use a transparent, concise, and goal-oriented approach. This could involve outlining the objectives at the beginning of the presentation, using bullet points to emphasize key information, and focusing on outcomes or solutions. Conversely, for an audience that values relational communication (often associated with feminine communication styles), incorporating storytelling, asking rhetorical questions to stimulate thought and discussion, and providing opportunities for audience participation can be more effective. These strategies cater to the audience's preferences and enhance your presentation's overall impact by aligning with their communication values.

Analyzing case studies where speakers have successfully navigated gender communication preferences can provide valuable insights into the practical applications of these strategies. Consider a scenario where a tech company executive presents a new product to a mixed-gender audience. The executive uses a balanced approach by starting with concise, data-driven points that appeal to a more assertive communication style, then weaving in customer testimonials and team stories that illustrate the collaborative efforts behind the product. This approach conveys the product's technical specifications and the human element of teamwork and customer satisfaction, catering to direct and relational communication preferences.

Another example could involve a healthcare conference where a keynote speaker addresses an audience of medical professionals. The speaker integrates gender-sensitive communication by highlighting statistics and evidence-based practices (appealing to a more direct style) and facilitating breakout sessions where participants discuss these practices in small groups to foster collaboration and consensus (appealing to a relational style). This dual approach ensures the presentation is robust, informative, interactive and inclusive.

Through these examples, it becomes evident that understanding and adapting to gender-specific communication styles is not about reinforcing stereotypes but recognizing and respecting how people communicate and perceive information. Employing strategies that embrace this diversity will enhance your effectiveness as a speaker, ensuring your presentations are heard and resonate deeply with every audience member.

Cultural Sensitivity

In today's globalized world, the ability to effectively communicate across cultural boundaries is not just an asset but a necessity for professional speakers. When you stand to deliver a speech or presentation to an international audience, your sensitivity to cultural nuances can dramatically affect the reception of your message. Building cultural awareness involves more than understanding surface-level differences; it requires a deep appreciation of the values, communication styles, and societal norms that shape how people perceive and process information. This awareness is critical, as it informs every aspect of your presentation, from the examples you choose to illustrate points to the stories you tell to connect with your audience.

To ensure your content resonates with a diverse audience, you must adapt it to reflect cultural relevance and respect. This adaptation process begins with thorough research into the cultural background of your audience. Understand the significant cultural influences, historical contexts, and current issues that may impact how your message is received. For instance, when presenting a new technology in a country with significant technological disparities, consider framing your message to acknowledge these gaps while highlighting the benefits of bridging them.

Adapting your content for cultural relevance means being mindful of local customs and sensitivities—avoid metaphors and analogies that may not translate well across cultures and replace them with locally relevant examples.

Consider the case of a multinational corporation that launched a series of workshops to facilitate better communication between its European and Asian branches. The workshops were designed with a deep understanding of the distinct communication styles prevalent in each region—direct in Europe versus subtle and indirect in Asia. The facilitators adapted their delivery to suit these styles, using clear and concise language for the European participants while employing more nuanced and context-driven explanations for the Asian attendees.

Another example I witnessed involved a global health organization that conducted public health campaigns in multiple countries to raise awareness about diabetes. Recognizing the cultural factors influencing dietary habits and health perceptions in different regions, the campaign managers tailored their messages to align with local values and beliefs. In some areas, this meant focusing on the impact of diabetes on family health, leveraging the family-centric solid values of the target audience. In others, the campaigns emphasized individual health and well-being, resonating with cultures prioritizing personal achievement and success.

Throughout these campaigns, the organizers carefully respected local traditions and customs, using culturally appropriate symbols and language to foster a greater connection with the audience.

These case studies highlight the importance of being culturally aware and adaptable, qualities that are indispensable in today's interconnected world.

Age-Specific Groups

When addressing an audience, the effectiveness of your communication can often hinge on how well you adapt your delivery to match your listeners' age-specific characteristics and preferences. This approach ensures that each audience segment receives your message in the most accessible and engaging manner possible.

For children with shorter attention spans and a developing understanding, the key is simplifying complex concepts and delivering them engagingly and dynamically. Utilize visual aids like colorful charts and images or incorporate props to make the learning experience more tangible. Storytelling is another powerful tool; weaving educational content into stories captures children's attention and conveys information in a naturally engaging format. It's also crucial to use language that is clear, straightforward, and devoid of complex jargon. Keep your sentences short and your terminology simple. When providing examples or scenarios, tie them to environments familiar to children, such as school activities or famous cartoons, making the abstract more concrete and relatable.

Transitioning to teenagers, often characterized by a quest for identity and a desire to be treated as adults, requires a different approach. Make your content relevant to their lives by discussing social media trends, educational challenges, or current events that resonate with their experiences. Foster an interactive environment by encouraging questions and discussions, keeping them engaged and feeling valued and understood. Adopting a respectful yet conversational tone is beneficial when communicating with teenagers and recognizing their growing maturity. Emphasize technology and multimedia in your presentations, as most teenagers are digital natives and respond positively to content delivered through these mediums.

Addressing seniors, on the other hand, calls for a shift in pace and clarity. Deliver your content more slowly to accommodate any cognitive processing needs and ensure that your speech is loud and clear, avoiding slang or idioms that may be unfamiliar or confusing. Focus on topics especially relevant to seniors, such as health care, retirement planning, or leisure activities that align with their interests and lifestyle. Acknowledging their vast experiences is also respectful; encouraging them to share their insights or relate their experiences to the topic at hand enriches the discussion and fosters a greater connection with them.

Audiences with Disabilities

When presenting to an audience that includes individuals with disabilities, it's essential to make your presentation accessible and inclusive. Here are some strategies to accommodate common disabilities:

1. Visual Impairments: provide large-print handouts or electronic copies of materials that can be easily magnified. Use high-contrast colors and legible fonts in your visual aids. Describe images, charts, and other visuals verbally for those who cannot see them. Ensure the presentation space has adequate lighting and minimal glare.

2. Hearing Impairments: use captioning or provide a written transcript of your presentation. Face the audience when speaking and keep your mouth visible for those who rely on lip reading. Use a microphone to amplify your voice and repeat questions from the audience before answering. Provide sign language interpretation, if possible, and when requested in advance.

3. Mobility Impairments: ensure the presentation venue is accessible, with ramps, elevators, and wide doorways. Arrange seating to accommodate wheelchairs and other mobility devices. Ensure the stage or speaking area is accessible with a ramp or lift. Allow for frequent breaks and provide a comfortable, accessible seating area.

4. Cognitive and Learning Disabilities: break complex information into smaller, more manageable chunks. Provide visual aids and

written materials to reinforce key points. Allow extra time for processing information and answering questions. Be patient, respectful, and willing to clarify or repeat information.

By implementing these strategies and being open to individual accommodations, you can create a more inclusive and accessible presentation environment that enables all audience members to engage fully with your message.

Engaging an Online Audience

In today's increasingly digital landscape, delivering effective virtual presentations is crucial for any public speaker. While virtual presentations come with their own unique set of challenges, there are several strategies you can employ to capture and maintain the attention of your online audience.

One of the most important aspects of virtual presenting is ensuring that your setup is optimized for engagement. This includes positioning your webcam at eye level to create the illusion of direct eye contact, ensuring that your face is well-lit with a soft, diffused light source, and selecting a clean, uncluttered background that won't distract from your message. By arranging your physical space properly, you'll be better equipped to connect with your audience and confidently deliver your content.

In addition to your physical setup, leveraging the tools and features available on your chosen webinar platform is essential. Encourage your audience to submit questions via the Q&A feature and use the chat box to foster discussion and gather feedback. For more intimate conversations or collaborative activities, use breakout rooms to facilitate small group interaction and exchange ideas.

When delivering your presentation, speaking directly to the camera and maintaining eye contact as if talking to someone in person is essential. Pay close attention to your body language and facial expressions; these nonverbal cues convey your message and enthusiasm. If you plan to share your screen, ensure that your slides or visuals are clear, legible, and visually appealing, avoiding the temptation to clutter your slides with too much text.

To create a truly immersive and memorable experience for your virtual audience, consider incorporating interactive elements such as polls, quizzes, or collaborative whiteboards. These tools encourage active participation and help break up the monotony of a traditional presentation format. Additionally, feel free to experiment with virtual backgrounds that align with your topic or brand, as this can help transport your audience and add a professional touch to your presentation.

Inevitably, technical issues or delays may arise during your virtual presentation. A backup plan is crucial, such as having your presentation offline or being prepared to switch to a different platform if necessary. By anticipating potential challenges and having contingency plans ready, you can navigate any obstacles gracefully and minimize disruptions to your audience's experience.

Ultimately, the key to mastering virtual presentations lies in your ability to adapt to the unique demands of the digital format while still connecting with your audience on a personal level. By implementing these strategies and continually refining your approach, you'll be well-positioned to deliver engaging virtual presentations.

Audience Adaptation Scenarios

I have created the following activity to encourage you to think critically about audience adaptation. It involves applying the techniques discussed in the chapter to realistic speaking situations. I have listed various speaking scenarios below.

For each one, outline a brief strategy for adapting your presentation to suit the needs of the relevant audience.

1. You're presenting a new technology product to:

-A group of senior citizens at a community center
-A room full of tech-savvy millennials at a startup incubator

2. You're giving a speech on climate change to:

-An international conference with attendees from various cultures
-A high school science class

3. You're delivering a workshop on leadership skills to:

-A mixed-gender group of corporate executives
-A group of young women in a mentorship program

4. You're presenting a new health initiative via a webinar to:

-Healthcare professionals from around the world
-Local community members with varying levels of health literacy

5. You're giving a presentation on financial planning to:

-An audience that includes individuals with visual impairments
-A group of recent college graduates

As you can see from this chapter, public speaking demands a deep understanding of your audience and the ability to adapt your approach to meet their diverse needs. We've explored various strategies for tailoring your presentations to different audiences, technical expertise, gender, culture, age, and physical abilities.

The key takeaway is that effective communication is more than one-size-fits-all. By recognizing the unique characteristics of your audience and adjusting your content and delivery accordingly, you can significantly enhance the impact of your message. Whether you're addressing a group of visual learners, bridging the gap between technical and non-technical listeners, navigating cultural sensitivities in international speeches, or engaging an online audience, your flexibility and adaptability as a speaker will set you apart.

These specialized techniques are not about stereotyping or making assumptions but about being attuned to any group's needs and preferences. By consistently striving to understand and connect with your audience on a deeper level, you'll improve the effectiveness of your presentations and foster a more inclusive and engaging environment for all participants.

As you continue to develop your public speaking skills, challenge yourself to step outside your norm and experiment with different approaches. Embrace the opportunity to learn from each audience interaction and use these experiences to refine your techniques further.

With practice and dedication, you'll become a versatile speaker capable of captivating and inspiring audiences across all walks of life.

12

PURSUING GROWTH AS A PUBLIC SPEAKER

"Communication works for those who work at it." J Powell

This chapter guides you through the evolving landscape of your speaking skills. Understanding and accepting the stages of change everyone goes through when learning something new is pivotal here. You'll discover how to navigate and thrive through these phases, setting realistic goals and cultivating resilience that transforms challenges into stepping stones for success.

When learning any new skill, people typically progress through four stages.[1] Initially, you're unaware of what you don't know—this is unconscious incompetence. As you begin to understand the complexities of the new skill, you enter conscious incompetence, recognizing your limitations. With practice, you reach conscious competence. Finally, after substantial experience, you achieve unconscious competence, speaking effectively without thinking about it. Recognizing these stages can help you stay motivated and understand that improvement will come with persistence and practice.

---

1. The four stages appeared in the 1960 textbook *Management of Training Programs* by three management professors at New York University. Management trainer Martin M. Broadwell called the model "the four levels of teaching" in an article published in February 1969. Paul R. Curtiss and Phillip W. Warren mentioned the model in their 1973 book *The Dynamics of Life Skills Coaching*. The model was used at Gordon Training International by its employee Noel Burch in the 1970s; there it was called the "four stages for learning any new skill".

The Learning Curve

Becoming a great public speaker is like climbing a series of hills; each ascent offers new views of proficiency and insight. Initially, you might grapple with the basics—overcoming nerves, mastering timing, and engaging your audience. This stage, often fraught with challenges, is where you lay the foundational skills upon which your future speaking talent will build. As you climb further, you encounter intermediate challenges, such as refining your storytelling techniques and using body language effectively. Each stage requires different strategies and mindsets, and recognizing where you are in this sequence is crucial.

Growth inherently involves stepping out of your comfort zone and embracing the discomfort of trying new things. Whether experimenting with a different presentation style, injecting humor into your speeches, or speaking to larger, more diverse audiences, each new experience can induce a sense of unease. This discomfort, however, is a powerful indicator of personal development. It signifies that you are pushing the boundaries of your known capabilities and venturing into new realms of potential.

To effectively manage and embrace this discomfort, start acknowledging it as an everyday learning process. Reframe these feelings as signs of growth rather than threats to your confidence. Remembering that this learning curve is not a straight path but a series of ebbs and flows will help maintain your motivation and commitment to continuous improvement.

Setting Exciting Goals

As you work through the stages of learning, setting realistic goals becomes your roadmap, guiding your journey and providing benchmarks for success. You may have heard of SMART goals. This is a method whereby your goals should be Specific, Measurable, Attainable, Relevant, and Time-bound. Here's an example:

Specific: Deliver ten paid speaking engagements on digital marketing to audiences of at least 100 people each.

Measurable: Track the number of engagements delivered, audience size, and income generated from speaking fees.

Achievable: Leverage existing network and gradually build reputation through smaller events to reach more extensive paid engagements.

Relevant: Aligns with career objectives as a public speaker and digital marketing expert.

Time-bound: Accomplish this goal within the next 12 months.

One day, I was walking my dog and thinking about my speaking goals; in my mind's eye, I saw the word 'SMART' backward, which reads 'TRAMS.' I started to think of my public speaking career as a journey. I visualized myself in the driver's seat of a tramcar. I pictured where I wanted to go and which companies I needed to speak to. I had a clear map to guide me in the right direction and a timetable to keep me moving forward. The passengers onboard were my support team, encouraging me to keep going when steep hills seemed impossible to climb. Now, I use my 'TRAMS'™ goal-setting method for everything I wish to achieve. Here's what each letter of the acronym stands for.

Towards: focus on moving forward towards your goal; don't look back.

Relationships: don't try to do everything on your own. Build a team around you. We all need supporters, mentors, speaking agencies, and colleagues who will recommend us.

Attitude: organisations want someone flexible and willing to work alongside their agenda. A positive attitude is everything when it comes to being hired as a speaker.

Meaningful: I want my speaking engagements to be meaningful and memorable for both the audience and me. Finding meaning in my work is very important, so I ensure this is included in all my goals and speeches.

Smile: the thought of every goal should excite you and make you smile. As mentioned in the chapter on body language, this is one vocabulary everyone understands and should be the first thing people see when you step on stage.

Take a moment now and write your TRAMS™ goals. Here are a few suggestions to help you:

Towards:
-Improve delivery skills and confidence
-Develop a more engaging speaking style
-Master various speech structures and formats
-Enhance ability to connect with diverse audiences

Relationships:
-Build rapport with audience members quickly
-Learn to read and respond to audience reactions
-Develop networking skills within speaking circles
-Collaborate effectively with event organizers and fellow speakers

Attitude:
-Cultivate a positive mindset before and during speeches
-Embrace constructive feedback as a growth opportunity
-Maintain composure under pressure
-Develop resilience in the face of setbacks or demanding audiences

Meaningful:
-Craft speeches that resonate with and inspire listeners
-Incorporate personal stories and experiences effectively
-Research thoroughly to provide valuable content
-Align speaking topics with personal values and passions

Smile:
-Use appropriate facial expressions to enhance delivery
-Practice genuine smiling to connect with the audience
-Incorporate humor to lighten the mood when appropriate
-Maintain a pleasant demeanor throughout presentations

You will want to adjust your goals as you evolve. What seemed a stretch goal when you started will soon become the norm, requiring you to set new, more challenging objectives. I encourage you to strive for continual improvement.

Persistence and Resilience

The path to public speaking excellence can be littered with setbacks—speeches that don't go as planned, audiences that don't engage, and feedback that is difficult to hear. Persistence in the face of these setbacks, powered by a resilient mindset, will see you through to success. Resilience in this context means more than just bouncing back; it involves learning from each experience, adapting your strategies, and persisting with renewed vigor.

Developing this resilience can be helped by viewing upsets as invaluable learning opportunities rather than criticisms of your ability. Create a support network of fellow speakers who understand your challenges and can provide insight and encouragement. Remember to celebrate your progress, no matter how small, as acknowledging growth fosters a positive mindset. Continuous improvement is not just about refining your skills but about redefining your potential. Each step forward updates the narrative of your public speaking journey.

Personal Practice Plan

Setting goals and having a plan is one thing, executing that plan and making those goals a reality is something else. In other words, developing your skills hinges not just on the knowledge you acquire but on how you apply this knowledge through deliberate practice. This plan is not merely a schedule; it is a strategic approach to honing your abilities, pinpointing areas for improvement, and consistently pushing the boundaries of your comfort zone.

It is essential to commit to this plan once created. Don't let anyone or anything get in the way of your practice plan; be determined, remain focused, make a promise to yourself, and you will reap the benefits.

The first step in developing this plan is assessing your current speaking skills. This process involves more than introspection; it requires honest and sometimes challenging feedback from trusted colleagues, mentors, or a professional coach. Utilize video recordings of your speeches or presentations to revisit your performance. Watch for flaws and subtler elements like pace, tone, and audience engagement. Are you speaking too quickly when nervous? Do you rely too heavily on your notes? Maybe your strengths lie in your ability to tell compelling stories, but you need help using non-verbal cues effectively. You create a baseline to build your practice plan by identifying these areas.

To truly improve your public speaking skills, it is essential to practice in a variety of scenarios. Each setting, from a formal business conference to an informal team meeting, offers unique challenges and opportunities for growth. Seek out these opportunities actively; volunteer to speak at local community events or offer to lead meetings at work. This variety will help improve your adaptability and build resilience as you adjust your delivery and content to suit different audiences and contexts. Also, consider practicing under less-than-ideal conditions. For example, you might practice speaking in a noisy environment to prepare for unexpected distractions during a presentation.

Keeping track of your progress is vital as it motivates you and provides insight into the effectiveness of your practice strategies. Create a simple log or journal where you record each practice session and note what went well and what didn't. Include details such as the date, the type of speaking engagement, the audience, and personal reflections. Over time, these entries will highlight patterns and trends, showing you where you've improved and where further practice is needed.

Revisit your goals periodically to assess whether they align with your development needs or should be adjusted. This ongoing process of tracking and tweaking ensures that your practice plan remains dynamic and aligned with your evolving skills and objectives.

Seeking Constructive Feedback

Feedback, often seen as daunting, is essential to unlocking profound growth and mastery in public speaking. For you, as a dedicated professional striving to enhance your oratory skills, establishing a productive feedback loop is vital. This involves gathering insights from various sources, understanding them, and implementing them effectively while maintaining emotional resilience. Let's explore how you can transform feedback into a powerful tool for your development.

The first step in establishing a productive feedback loop is actively reaching out to those who have witnessed your presentations—peers, mentors, or audience members—and asking for their honest insights. It's essential to approach this with a specific request; rather than asking whether your presentation was 'good' or 'bad,' encourage detailed comments on aspects such as your delivery, the clarity of your message, or the effectiveness of your visuals. You can facilitate this process by creating structured opportunities for feedback. For instance, after a presentation, you might distribute a quick survey that asks specific questions about various elements of your performance. Alternatively, consider a more informal approach, like inviting a peer for a coffee discussion to reflect on your latest speaking event. Whichever method you choose, the key is to make it easy for people to provide their observations and insights in a way that is structured enough to be helpful but open enough to encourage honest, constructive criticism.

I like to use the following questions.

Questions to Elicit Feedback:

1. What were the key takeaways from my presentation?

2. How well did I communicate my main points?

3. What parts of my presentation resonated with you the most?

4. Were there any areas where I could have provided more clarity or detail?

5. How effective were my visuals and supporting materials?

6. Did my delivery style (e.g., tone, pacing, body language) enhance or detract from my message?

7. What are your suggestions for improving my content, delivery, or audience engagement?

Analyzing Feedback

Once you've gathered feedback, the next challenge is analyzing it to extract actionable insights. This stage is crucial and requires a balanced approach; it's easy to focus on overwhelmingly positive or negative feedback, but actual growth comes from a comprehensive analysis considering all perspectives. Start by compiling the feedback and looking for common themes. If multiple people noted that your speech was inspiring but too detailed, consider how to maintain your motivational edge while simplifying the content. It's also beneficial to categorize the feedback into content, delivery, and audience interaction. This helps you identify which aspects of your speaking are most vital and which need more attention.

To deepen your understanding, cross-reference the feedback with your self-assessment and perhaps video recordings of your performance. Seeing yourself through the lens of your audience can provide new perspectives and highlight discrepancies between your self-perception and how others perceive you. This analysis is not just about identifying flaws but also about recognizing and reinforcing your strengths, which are very valuable for building confidence as a speaker.

Separating Self from Critique

Critique, a word that often sends shivers down the spine of many professionals, is not just a tool to foster improvement but a gateway to profound personal and professional growth. For you, as a public speaker striving to enhance your efficacy and impact, understanding how to process and learn from critique without undermining your confidence is crucial. This involves a delicate balance of detaching your identity from the critique, cultivating a mindset that sees feedback as positive, engaging in constructive self-talk, and leveraging the guidance of mentors.

The art of receiving critique begins with the understanding that feedback on your performance does not reflect your worth as an individual. It's about your actions or delivery, not your identity. To navigate this, start by framing critique as data—neutral, impersonal information you can use to decide how to adjust your behavior or approach. This perspective shift is vital in maintaining objectivity and preventing emotional responses that can cloud judgment or damage self-esteem. For instance, if someone critiques your presentation skills, interpret this as specific to the situation and not as an indication of your overall capabilities. Practicing this separation consistently can transform potentially hurtful experiences into opportunities for growth, allowing you to approach feedback with curiosity rather than defensiveness.

Cultivating a Growth Mindset

Central to learning from critique is cultivating a growth mindset—believing your abilities can be developed through dedication and hard work. Instead of a fixed mindset that sees skills as static and unchangeable, this mindset empowers you to view critique as a necessary part of learning. Embrace the idea that each piece of feedback is a stepping stone to greater mastery and that setbacks are not a sign of failure but a part of the learning process. Embedding this philosophy into your practice involves regular reflection on how you respond to feedback and consciously choosing to see each critique as a chance to evolve. For instance, after each speaking event, instead of focusing solely on what went wrong, ask yourself, "What can I learn from this?" and "How can this help me improve?" This approach enhances your resilience and keeps you motivated and engaged in your developmental journey.

Constructive Self-Talk

Your dialogue with yourself in response to critique can either be a powerful tool for growth or a destructive force that impedes your progress. Negative self-talk, where you might tell yourself that you're not good enough and you'll never improve, can erode your confidence and skew your perception of your abilities. To counter this, engage in constructive self-talk that is supportive and objective. Replace critical thoughts with affirmations and statements that encourage learning and improvement. For example, if you think, "I messed up that presentation," reframe it to, "I have an opportunity to learn from this." Another good one is, "I am proud of myself for stepping up and facing the challenge, regardless of the outcome." By consciously adjusting your internal narrative, you reinforce a positive self-image and build resilience against the potentially disheartening effects of critical feedback.

Finding Mentors and Coaches

Navigating the critique terrain can be significantly enhanced by the guidance of a mentor or coach who can provide expert feedback and emotional support. These individuals act as sounding boards, offering perspectives and insights you might not know. They can help you see your blind spots, interpret feedback constructively, and implement changes effectively. Additionally, mentors serve as models of receiving and using critique positively, providing real-life examples of resilience and adaptability. Establishing relationships with mentors involves reaching out to experienced individuals whom you respect and whose feedback you value. Regularly engage with them to discuss your progress, challenges, and feedback you've received, and be open to their guidance and suggestions.

Through these strategies—separating your self-worth from critique, fostering a growth mindset, practicing constructive self-talk, and engaging with mentors—you create a robust framework for turning critique into a dynamic personal and professional development tool. This structure facilitates your growth as a speaker and enriches your resilience, ensuring your confidence remains intact and even strengthened through every feedback you encounter. As you continue to implement these practices, remember that each critique is not just a reflection of where you are but a signpost pointing toward where you can go, offering insights essential for your journey of continuous improvement and success in public speaking.

Peer Review Groups

In public speaking, where personal improvement is as crucial as the applause at the end of a speech, peer review holds great value. Engaging with a group of fellow speakers who review each other's practices not only enhances individual skills but also fosters a community of continuous learning. Forming or joining a peer review group can seem daunting, but its benefits are profound. Start by reaching out within your existing networks—professional associations, speaking clubs, or even among workplace colleagues who share a keen interest in refining their public speaking abilities. The goal is to gather a diverse group of individuals who bring varying levels of expertise and perspectives to the table, as this diversity will enrich the feedback and learning experiences for all members.

When forming these groups, it's essential to establish clear guidelines that underscore the importance of constructive and respectful feedback. It is necessary that all group members feel safe and valued, as this will encourage open and honest communication. As mentioned earlier, effective peer reviews should focus on specific aspects of speaking, such as delivery, content clarity, and audience engagement, rather than veering into personal critiques that can be discouraging. It's also beneficial to rotate the roles of speaker and reviewer within the group, ensuring that each member receives balanced feedback and the opportunity to observe and critique others. This rotation not only enhances the learning experience but also keeps the group both dynamic and engaging.

Balancing the art of giving and receiving feedback within these groups is essential. When receiving feedback, approach it with an open mind, recognizing that each piece of feedback is a gift that provides insights into how you can improve. Conversely, when giving feedback, do so with kindness and precision. Aim to be specific in your critiques and always offer suggestions for improvement. For instance, instead of saying, "Your speech was unclear," you might say, "I think your message would be clearer if you outlined your main points at the beginning." This specific feedback is more valuable to the speaker and demonstrates a supportive approach to peer review.

You'll often find the advice you give is just as applicable to your own practice. Moreover, discussing different approaches and techniques within the group can spark new ideas and inspire you to try techniques you might not have considered before.

Remember to celebrate your successes along the way and embrace the ongoing journey of growth and development as a speaker. With dedication, perseverance, and a commitment to continuous learning, you'll unlock your full potential as an influential communicator and thought leader.

13

SETTING YOURSELF APART AS A PUBLIC SPEAKER

"The world says fit in; the universe says stand out."
M Dhliwayo

Every speaker brings a distinct set of traits to the podium, and understanding these can transform your public speaking from standard to standout. Personality assessments like the Myers-Briggs Type Indicator (MBTI), DISC, or the Big Five personality traits provide insightful frameworks for understanding your natural talents. Are you an extrovert who thrives on interaction or an introvert who excels in thoughtful deliberation? Do you respond to stress with a calm pragmatism, or do you harness the energy of stressful situations to enhance your dynamism? Understanding these aspects of your personality can help reveal your inherent strengths and potential weaknesses as a speaker.

Personality undeniably shapes every facet of our behavior and interactions; public speaking is no exception. The nuances of your personality influence how you perceive and are perceived by your audience, impacting everything from your choice of words to your body language. For instance, an extroverted speaker might naturally enjoy engaging with large audiences, thriving on the direct feedback and energy of the crowd. In contrast, an introverted speaker might excel in delivering detailed, thoughtful presentations to smaller groups where a more profound connection can be formed. Understanding this intrinsic link between personality types and speaking styles is crucial for leveraging your strengths and addressing any inherent challenges.

Adapting your natural speaking style to meet various audiences starts with a keen awareness of your personality traits. This awareness is not about altering who you are but optimizing your approach to communication in different contexts. For example, suppose you are naturally introverted and must engage a large audience. In that case, you might incorporate more structured audience interaction into your presentation, such as planned Q&A sessions, to help manage and direct audience engagement more comfortably. Conversely, if an extrovert needs to engage in more detailed and nuanced discussions, practice focusing your energy on listening and providing thoughtful responses rather than dominating the conversation. This adaptability broadens your effectiveness as a speaker and significantly enhances your audience's experience by ensuring that your delivery method matches the content and setting.

Persuasive Techniques

The ability to persuade effectively is about delivering a message and moving your audience to action. This requires a deep understanding of the principles of persuasion: ethos, pathos, and logos. Ethos refers to the credibility of the speaker. By establishing yourself as a credible source, you gain the trust of your audience, making them more open to your message. Conversely, pathos appeals to the audience's emotions, tapping into their values, desires, and fears to create a connection that transcends the intellectual content of your speech. Lastly, logos involves the logical structure of your argument, ensuring your points are coherent, well-supported, and compelling.

Building credibility, or ethos, begins long before you step onto the stage. It starts with your reputation and the respect you command in your field. However, within the context of your presentation, credibility is often established in how you introduce your topic and yourself. It's about demonstrating your expertise and authority on the subject. This can be achieved by citing relevant qualifications, experiences, or even anecdotes highlighting your depth of knowledge and commitment to the field. Moreover, the clarity and confidence of your delivery play a crucial role; a speaker who seems unsure or unfamiliar with their material will quickly lose the audience's trust. Therefore, thorough preparation and a deep understanding of your topic are fundamental.

The key lies in understanding your audience's values and emotional triggers regarding pathos or emotional appeal. This requires a nuanced approach, as what moves one audience may not resonate with another. Your message's emotional core should align with your audience's interests and passions. For instance, if you are addressing a group of entrepreneurs, emphasizing themes of innovation, risk-taking, and the thrill of building something new can be particularly effective. Emotional appeal can also be strengthened through personal stories or vivid descriptions that allow the audience to visualize the impact of your message on real life. These stories should be chosen carefully to evoke specific emotions such as empathy, pride, or even righteous anger, driving the audience to feel deeply about the subject, which is crucial to motivating action.

Crafting a compelling call to action is the culmination of your persuasive efforts. This part of your speech must be clear, urgent, and feasible, providing the audience with concrete steps to take in response to your message. The effectiveness of your call to action depends significantly on how well you've managed to establish credibility and evoke emotions. It should feel like a natural next step, an opportunity for the audience to act on the feelings and convictions your speech has inspired. For example, suppose your goal is to persuade your company to adopt a new sustainability initiative. In that case, your call to action might involve inviting your audience to join a pilot project or attend a workshop on the initiative.

Whatever the action, it should be framed so that the audience feels empowered and eager to participate, seeing it as a way to be part of a solution or movement that aligns with their values and emotions discussed throughout your presentation.

Incorporating these elements of persuasion into your speeches transforms them from mere presentations of ideas into powerful calls to action that have the potential to inspire and mobilize your audience. As you continue to refine these techniques, remember that the goal of persuasion is not just to convince but to connect, not just to argue but to inspire. Each speech is an opportunity to share knowledge, forge relationships, and create movements reflecting your audience's aspirations and values. Mastering this skill will help you rise above the norm.

Using Humor to Differentiate

Incorporating humor into your public speaking can significantly enhance the engagement and memorability of your presentations, transforming even the most mundane topics into delightful entertainment for your audience. Understanding the various types of humor and their strategic application is crucial for ensuring that your humorous content resonates well and contributes positively to your objectives.

Humor comes in many forms, each serving different purposes within public speaking. Anecdotal humor, for example, involves personal stories or observations that are amusing and relatable, making your presentation more personable and down-to-earth. On the other hand, situational humor arises from the context or circumstances described during the speech, offering a light-hearted take on potentially complex or dry subjects. Then, there's topical humor, which relates to current events or trends, connecting your speech to broader, contemporary themes. Each type of humor has its place and can be incredibly effective when matched appropriately with the topic and audience demographics.

However, the key to successfully incorporating humor lies in choosing the right type and mastering the timing and appropriateness of its use. Timing in humor is everything. A well-timed joke or humorous remark can serve as a perfect icebreaker or punctuate a section of your speech, providing a mental break for your audience. It's essential to deliver the punchline when it can be most appreciated – typically after a build-up of context or following a poignant point, giving the audience a chance to digest the information while enjoying a light-hearted moment.

Appropriateness, meanwhile, involves ensuring that the humor aligns with the audience's values and expectations and remains sensitive to diverse perspectives. This is particularly crucial in today's globalized world, where cultural sensitivities must be navigated carefully. Avoid humor that might be divisive or offensive, which can alienate parts of your audience and detract from your message. Instead, opt for inclusive and respectful humor, enhancing your rapport with the audience without undermining the seriousness of your topic when necessary.

Practicing the delivery of your humorous content is as important as the content itself. The impact of a funny story or joke often lies in the delivery – the timing, tone, facial expressions, and body language. Pay attention to your intonation and pacing, as these can dramatically affect how the humor is perceived. A backup plan is also beneficial; if a particular piece of humor does not seem to land as expected, be prepared to smoothly transition back into your main content without dwelling on the miss.

Analyzing examples of effective humorous speeches can provide valuable insights. Consider the speeches of professional speakers who skillfully integrate humor into their presentations. Observe how they set up an amusing story, the cues they use to signal a joke, and how they tie the humor back to the central message of their speech. Many seasoned speakers use humor to make complex information more accessible, to disarm the audience, or to refresh the attention span during longer sessions.

In your next presentation, try integrating humor by starting with small, safe jokes or universally relatable anecdotes. As you grow more comfortable and receive positive feedback, gradually introduce more nuanced humor that plays off the deeper content of your speech.

Remember, the goal of using humor is to entertain and create a memorable, engaging experience that enhances the audience's connection to your message and sets you apart from other speakers.

Building Your Brand

In the competitive arena of public speaking, your brand guides audiences and collaborators toward your unique message and style. Think of your brand as your professional signature—a blend of your experiences, expertise, values, and personality that you consistently present to the world.

Defining this brand requires introspection and strategy. It starts by asking yourself key questions: What am I passionate about? What do I want my audience to remember about me? What differentiates me from other speakers? The answers to these questions form the foundation of your brand, encapsulating what you stand for and how you wish to be perceived professionally.

As you hone this personal brand, consider how it enhances your public speaking endeavors. A strong, clear brand can transform the way your audience perceives you. It acts like a thread connecting diverse speaking engagements, ensuring your identity and message remain coherent and compelling, whether addressing an intimate seminar or a large conference. This consistency builds trust and amplifies your authority as a speaker. For example, if your brand is centered around innovative leadership, your presentation should echo this theme through content, speaking style, or the stories you share. This clear branding helps your audience understand and relate to your message more deeply, enhancing the impact of your presentations.

Consistency across all platforms is essential in today's digitally connected world. Your brand should be unmistakable, whether someone is viewing your LinkedIn profile or sitting in the audience at one of your talks. Each platform offers a unique opportunity to reinforce your brand attributes. Use social media to share insights and stories that reflect your brand, publish articles or blog posts that delve into your areas of expertise, and ensure that your visual branding—from the design of your PowerPoint presentations to your profile pictures—aligns with the brand you are building. This consistent presentation helps solidify your professional image and makes you more recognizable and relatable to your audience, fostering a sense of familiarity and loyalty.

Leveraging your brand effectively opens numerous doors for professional opportunities and engagements. Begin by identifying platforms and forums where your brand's message will most likely resonate. Engage actively with these platforms— industry conferences, workshops, or online webinars.

Networking plays a crucial role here. Connect with other professionals who share or value your brand attributes. This networking can lead to collaborative opportunities, speaking engagements, or guest appearances on podcasts and webinars that reach your target audience. Additionally, consider teaching or mentoring, which allows you to give back to the community and reinforces your position as an expert in your field. Each strategy extends your professional reach and embeds your brand more deeply in public speaking.

Your choice of dress and overall appearance is a powerful tool for reinforcing your brand. Every element, from clothing to accessories, should reflect your brand's attributes. If your brand emphasizes creativity and innovation, you might incorporate unique or artistic elements that signal creative thinking and modernity into your attire. Alternatively, classic styles and colors can subconsciously communicate these qualities to your audience if your brand is built on trust and reliability. This strategic alignment of appearance with the brand helps make a memorable impression and create a consistent image that audiences can relate to across different speaking engagements.

I know a motivational speaker who dresses in vibrant colors and eclectic patterns when addressing audiences at creative leadership conferences. This deliberate choice makes her instantly recognizable and mirrors her message of thinking outside the box and pushing boundaries. Her distinctive style complements her vibrant delivery and engaging content, making her presentations memorable and her brand distinctive. Audience feedback often highlights the inspiration they derive from her talks and how her appearance and energy make her messages more impactful and relatable.

A friend of mine who is a financial advisor speaks at retirement planning seminars and often opts for a conservative, meticulously tailored appearance that communicates trustworthiness and attention to detail—qualities highly valued in his field. His suit, tie, and overall grooming are chosen to project an image of stability and reliability, reinforcing his expertise in financial matters. Attendees at his seminars often note how his professional appearance made them more receptive to his advice on economic security and investments.

These examples underscore how effectively aligning your appearance with your speaking context and brand can significantly enhance your credibility and the impact of your message. They also illustrate that while content is paramount, visual elements, including your appearance, play a crucial role in how that content is perceived and received. Hence, thoughtful consideration of how you present yourself visually is not just about making a good impression—it's an integral part of your communication strategy that can amplify your influence and help you achieve your speaking goals.

Your brand is not just about how you are seen—it's about making an indelible mark on your audience, ensuring that your message reaches and resonates meaningfully.

Your Speaker Profile

Consistently using social media to share your speaking engagements, insights, and professional reflections can significantly enhance your profile as a speaker. Each post, share, or interaction contributes to building a knowledgeable, approachable persona and engaging with current trends and discussions. Highlighting your speaking engagements, sharing behind-the-scenes content, and discussing your preparation process can make your public persona more relatable and accessible, attracting more followers and enhancing your credibility.

Regularly update your social media profiles with upcoming speaking engagements, feedback from past events, and professional accolades. This keeps your audience informed and showcases your active involvement and success in the speaking arena. Engaging with other speakers, thought leaders, and professional groups on social media platforms can further broaden your network and influence.

By strategically leveraging social media before, during, and after your presentations, you transform each speaking engagement from a finite event into an ongoing conversation that continually enhances your relationship with your audience and strengthens your position as a thought leader. This dynamic interaction ensures that your message resonates far beyond the immediate confines of your presentation, creating lasting impact and ongoing engagement.

Organized and Prepared

The devil lies in the details when preparing for a public speaking engagement. Ensuring thorough preparation not only boosts your confidence but also significantly enhances the quality of your delivery. A meticulous preparation checklist is indispensable, serving as your roadmap through the myriad tasks that lead to a successful presentation.

Let's delve into what such a checklist should include, ensuring that every presentation aspect is polished and poised for success.

Firstly, the checklist should begin with a review of your speech objectives and audience analysis. This ensures that your content is aligned with the goals of the presentation and tailored to the audience's interests and needs. Following this, a detailed content review is crucial. This includes verifying facts, refining key messages, and ensuring a logical flow of ideas. Each of these steps helps construct a coherent and compelling narrative.

Next, consider the technical aspects—check the compatibility of your presentation with available equipment and familiarize yourself with the setup. This is particularly important to avoid last-minute hiccups that could disrupt your flow.

Another critical entry in your checklist should be the preparation of backup materials. This includes having extra copies of your speech, backup slides, and alternative equipment like clickers or adapters. Such foresight can be a lifesaver when technology fails or materials are misplaced. Lastly, set aside time for several dry runs of your presentation. These practice sessions are invaluable as they help you fine-tune your delivery, adjust your timing, and become comfortable with your material. This part of your checklist ensures that when you finally step onto the stage, you are familiar with your content and confident in your ability to deliver it effectively.

Public Speaker's Checklist

Before the Presentation:

1 Define the purpose and key message of your presentation

2. Analyze your audience and tailor your content accordingly

3. Develop a clear structure and outline for your presentation

4. Create engaging and visually appealing slides or materials

5. Rehearse your presentation multiple times, focusing on timing and delivery

6. Test all technical equipment (microphone, projector, computer) in advance

7. Arrive at the venue early to familiarize yourself with the space and setup

8. Ensure you have backup copies of your presentation materials

9. Dress appropriately for the occasion and audience

10. Take a few moments to relax, breathe, and center yourself before starting

During the Presentation:

1 Start with a strong opening that captures the audience's attention

2. Maintain eye contact with your audience, scanning the room

3. Use clear, concise language and avoid jargon or technical terms

4. Speak at an appropriate pace, allowing time for pauses and emphasis

5. Vary your tone, pitch, and volume to keep the audience engaged

6. Utilize gestures and body language to enhance your message

7. Incorporate storytelling, examples, and anecdotes to illustrate your points

8. Engage the audience with questions, polls, or interactive elements

9. Manage your time effectively, ensuring you cover all key points

10. Navigate any technical issues or disruptions calmly and professionally

After the Presentation:

1 Conclude with a robust and memorable closing that reinforces your main message

2. Invite the audience to ask questions and engage in discussion

3. Provide your contact information for follow-up questions or feedback

4. Thank the audience for their attention and participation

5. Gather feedback from the audience through surveys or informal conversations

6. Reflect on your performance, noting areas for improvement

7. Follow up with any promised resources or materials for the audience

8. Share your presentation slides or materials online if appropriate

9. Update your portfolio or website with any photos, videos, or testimonials from the event

10. Celebrate your success and use the experience to refine your skills for future presentations

Using this checklist, you can ensure that you are well-prepared, confident, and ready to deliver an engaging and impactful presentation while taking steps to improve your skills and grow as a speaker continuously.

Organizational Tools and Apps

Many digital tools and apps can help you organize and prepare for your presentations. These resources can streamline your preparation process, enhance productivity, and ensure you are fully equipped for your speech.

One such tool is Evernote, a versatile app that allows you to organize your research, draft your speeches, and store all your speaking notes in one accessible place. Its ability to sync across devices ensures you can work on your speech at your desk or on the go.

Another invaluable tool is Trello, which offers a visual overview of your preparation process through customizable boards, lists, and cards. This tool is handy for managing large projects or collaborating with a team, as it allows you to track the progress of each task and assign responsibilities.

For speakers who want to refine their delivery, tools like Orai come in handy. Orai provides detailed feedback on your pacing, clarity, and energy, allowing you to polish your delivery by identifying areas for improvement through AI-driven insights.

Choosing the correct set of tools that align with your needs ensures that every aspect of your speech, from content creation is meticulously crafted and ready for the stage.

If you get stuck at any stage in the process and would like assistance or coaching, get in touch with me, see QR code on page 166.

14

Final Word

"Speakers who talk about what life has taught them never fail to keep the attention of their listeners." D Carnegie.

I sincerely hope you have enjoyed this book and learned a lot. However, reading the advice on these pages is only the start. Putting what you have learned into practice is what will achieve success. I firmly believe anyone willing to put in the time and effort can learn and master the skill of public speaking. This powerful tool can open doors to countless personal and professional opportunities.

Throughout this book, we have explored the various aspects of public speaking, from the initial stages of overcoming stage fright and self-doubt to more advanced persuasion techniques and well-timed humor. We have seen how public speaking can inform and inspire, help individuals and organizations achieve their goals, and positively impact the world.

Storytelling is essential in public speaking, as it allows you to harness the power of narrative to make your messages more memorable. By weaving personal anecdotes, case studies, and metaphors into your presentations, you can create an emotional connection with your listeners, making them more receptive to your ideas and more likely to act based on your words.

Body language and nonverbal communication reinforce your message and help build rapport with your audience. By using confident, open postures, maintaining eye contact, and using gestures to emphasize key points, you can convey a sense of authority and enthusiasm that can be infectious.

Vocal techniques are another vital aspect of effective public speaking. Enhancing your vocal delivery through proper breathing, pacing, and intonation can captivate your audience and keep them engaged from start to finish. Whether speaking to a small group or a large auditorium, the ability to project your voice and vary your tone can make all the difference in how your message is received.

Effective use of technology and visual aids can also be a powerful tool in public speaking, particularly in today's digital age. By incorporating multimedia elements such as slides, videos, and interactive polls, you can create a more engaging and dynamic experience for your audience. However, it is essential to use these tools wisely and keep them from overshadowing the substance of your message.

Public speaking is not always painless, and there will inevitably be challenges and obstacles along the way. Handling challenging situations with poise and confidence is a hallmark of a skilled public speaker. Whether navigating tough questions, managing interruptions, or dealing with difficult audience members, remaining calm and composed under pressure is crucial to maintaining credibility and authority.

I'm sure you will agree that one of the key takeaways from this book is the importance of authenticity and finding your unique speaking style. By embracing your strengths, passions, and experiences, you can develop a genuine, relatable, and compelling speaking persona. This authenticity allows you to connect with your audience on a human level, building trust and rapport that can lead to lasting relationships and ongoing opportunities.

Ultimately, the key to setting yourself apart as a public speaker is continually striving for growth and improvement. You can become a more confident, effective communicator by seeking feedback, setting goals, and consistently practicing your skills. This may involve stepping outside your comfort zone, trying new techniques, and learning from your mistakes, but the rewards of becoming a skilled public speaker are well worth the effort.

So go out confidently, let your voice be heard, and know that your words can change lives. The journey of a thousand miles begins with a single step, and by taking that first step into the world of public speaking, you are embarking on a path of growth, discovery, and endless possibility.

I'm excited for you!

Anne

PS: Whether you're preparing for a big presentation, aiming to improve your pitch, or just looking to feel more comfortable speaking in public, I can help you. I offer personalized coaching tailored to your specific needs and goals. Scan the QR code below to get in touch and let's talk.

Make a Difference with Your Review
Unlock the Power of Public Speaking

Kindness is never wasted; it always makes a difference. B De Angelis

Public speaking is a skill that can transform your and your audience's lives. But something even more powerful binds this world together: the magic of sharing. Just as your words can inspire, so can your voice make a positive difference.

My aim with "*Public Speaking: From Stage Fright to Spotlight*" is simple: to make the transformative power of public speaking accessible to all. The only way to truly accomplish this is to spread the word.

And that's where your voice comes into play—most people judge a book by its cover, but even more by its reviews.

Would you be kind enough to leave a review of this book for the aspiring speaker, the eager learner, or the curious reader you've never met?

Your review, which will take no more than one minute, could...

...ignite a passion in a young communicator.
...inspire a professional to enhance their speaking skills.
...help an educator find a resource for their students.
...bring together communities through powerful stories.
...make one more person step confidently onto the stage.

If the magic of sharing resonates with you, you truly understand the spirit of public speaking. Welcome to the world of effective communication. Scan QR code on next page to leave your review. You're one of us!

With immense gratitude,

Anne

Scan the QR code below to leave your review.

USA

AUSTRALIA

UK

www.ingramcontent.com/pod-product-compliance
Lightning Source LLC
Chambersburg PA
CBHW072005290426
44109CB00018B/2136